A Day with the Shama

A Day with the Shama

Essays on Nature

S. Theodore Baskaran

ZERO DEGREE PUBLISHING

A Day With The Shama ©2020 S.Theodore Baskaran
First Edition : July 2020
By ZERO DEGREE PUBLISHING

ISBN: 978-93-88860-80-2
ZDP Title : 30

ZERO DEGREE PUBLISHING
No.55(7), R Block, 6th Avenue,
Anna Nagar,
Chennai - 600 040

Website: www.zerodegreepublishing.com
E Mail id: zerodegreepublishing@gmail.com
Phone : +91 98400 65000

Cover Design : Boopathy Srinivasan
Typeset : Vidhya Velayudham
Clipart : Vecteezy.com

with love to

Mateo
and his generation

Contents

Introduction

It was in the winter of 1969, I published by first article after watching a skein of Bar-headed geese land in a lake near Tiruchi. S V Krishnamurthy in *The Hindu* accepted the piece and encouraged me to write more. There were not many writings on nature at that time. M. Krishnan was publishing in the *Statesman*.

The arrival of two books, *The Wildlife of India* (1964) by E P Gee and *The Deer and the Tiger* (1967) created an awareness about wildlife, Following the Stockholm conference in 1972, environmental concerns came to be articulated and nature writing gained an importance. The Government of India took a series of steps, including the passing of the historic Wildlife Protection Act of 1972. In the 1970s and 80s, the professional wildlife biologists came on the scene. Magazines, though very few, devoted to wildlife began appearing. The hunting accounts of the Raj, which was our only source of natural history knowledge, soon became obsolete as sources of knowledge on natural history.

I wrote mainly on birds and birdwatching. However, soon my concern widened. I got interested in wildlife in general and you cannot write about animals without talking about their habitat-rivers, forests, scrub, seaside and so on and what is happening to these areas.

Being a civil servant I moved from place to place on transfer and this gave me opportunity to live in different parts of our country. One of the unforgettable experiences was spending a night in the village of Haflong in Assam, watching 'the bird suicide phenomenon.' My job provided opportunities to travel to other countries. I recall spending an hour hiding behind a bush at the Black Forest in Mauritius watching the rare Mauritian kestrel. I was able to spend some time in the sanctuaries at Masai Mara and Lake Nakuru while on a U N assignment in Kenya.

Broadly one can identify two types of nature writing. One is to write intuitively responding to nature and its myriad forms of expression, like Thoreau did in *Walden*, and the other is to look at wildlife from the point of view of a biologist, like Raman Sukumar has done. There are some rare writers who combine the two skills, like Peter Matthiessen.

In his book *The Birds of Heaven*, Matthiessen puts down his philosophy of wildlife writing "One way to grasp the main perspectives of environment and biodiversity is to understand the origins and precious nature of a single living form, a single manifestation of the miracle of existence; if one has truly understood a crane–or a leaf or a cloud or a frog- one has understood everything."

I wrote about my experience and how I reacted to a bird or a mammal or an issue. This book contains articles I had published in the last twenty years, mostly in *The Hindu*. I thank Nirmla Lakshman of *The Hindu* for giving permission to publish them in this book. I am grateful to the photographers for letting me use their pictures. I am grateful to Ramjee and Gayathri for so caringly seeing this book through.

'Amaravathi'

Bangalore

S.Theodore Baskaran

BIRDS

The Song Of The Shama

Dawn was just breaking over Karnala bird sanctuary. Sitting in that delightfully rudimentary roadside tea shop, I was nursing a thoughtful cup of tea and trying to recollect the direction given by my fellow birder to a good birding spot nearby. I crossed the road, walked a kilometre and came to a dry nullah at the foot of a small hill.

As I started climbing up, threading my way through a bridle path, I noticed the first few rays of the sun hit the treetops. Two racket-tailed drongos chased each other, as though settling a domestic quarrel. And then I heard the fluid long whistle, ending with a series of short yodelling notes.

I peered in that direction and scanned the bushes with my binoculars; at first, I could see only a spot of red. As I trained my binoculars, the dainty figure of a Shama resolved itself, set off clearly by a green background, sitting on a low bough and singing. After whistling a few bars it arched its tail up, hopped down to give a few tentative pecks among the leaves on the ground and was on its perch again.

The Shama, a black bird of bulbul size, is one of our most reputed singers, with an extensive repertoire and is truly a pride of our forests. It has a reddish abdomen and a long slightly forked tail. It was to see and listen to this bird that I had come to Karnala and I saw it exactly at the same spot to which I had been directed by my friend. It was as though he had sent a secret message to the Shama that I would be coming and should not return disappointed. Officially referred to as the White-rumped Shama, it is found in many spots in the Western Ghats. I have seen it near Baraliar, en route to Ooty. In Tamil, the bird has a picturesque name, *Solaibadi,* the one that sings in the Shola.

The Karnala Bird sanctuary is 80 kilometres from Mumbai on the road to Goa and covers an area of five square kilometres. Unlike most bird sanctuaries in the country—which are in marshes and are habitats of waterfowl like those in Bharatpur and Vedanthangal—the sanctuary at Karnala is a chunk of moist deciduous forest. This is the type of forest that once covered wide stretches of the Deccan plateau, providing an ideal theatre for the guerilla tactics of the Maratha forces against the British army during the nineteenth century. In fact, one of the measures the British took to contain the Maratha forces was to destroy vast areas of these forests, a primitive version of the defoliation programme brutally conducted by the American forces in Vietnam.

It must be remembered that all the sanctuaries for mammals also harbour and support a sizable bird population. In fact, the Manas sanctuary in Assam is also a great place for birds. But bird life in these sanctuaries does not offer any large and easy spectacle which could be viewed comfortably from an elephant's back or from inside a jeep. After walking long stretches in the woods, consider yourself lucky if you get a fleeting glimpse of a Heart-spotted woodpecker or can listen tantalizingly to the song of the Quaker babbler without being able to actually spot it.

The mammals in these sanctuaries—like the gaur in Mudumalai or the rhino in Kaziranga—steal the show and the birds do not get the notice they deserve even from conservationists. Here comes the importance of an exclusive sanctuary for birds of the forest. Salim Ali, in an interview, had said that the only way to save our birds — which mind you is more difficult than saving mammals because of their predilection to migration—is to ensure a proper habitat and guard them zealously. This is precisely what Karnala is for.

The Karnala fort, after which the sanctuary has been named, forms the backdrop at its eastern end and lends a tone as it were, to the place. The giant basalt pillar rock, known locally as Pandu's tower, rising vertically to a height of 50 metres, is a remnant of its volcanic past of the Deccan. It can be seen from any point in the sanctuary and helps to keep your bearings while roaming in the woods. The fort, commanding an important highway, was much sought-after by the warring chieftains till the middle of the nineteenth century. Now overgrown with shrubs, langurs and lizards keep the courts where Jamshyd gloried and drank deep.

A strongly recommended experience in Karnala is the eight kilometre walk to Ransai lake (outside the sanctuary limits) and back. Good birding all the way, Golden and Black-headed orioles, Paradise flycatchers and if you are lucky, even the shy and retiring Malabar trogon.

You pass through two tiny villages of Takur adivasis before arriving at the lake to see a colony of Weaver birds noisily engaged in nest-building, making sorties in batches to tear strands of paddy crops to build their pendulous nests. The migrants – sandpipers and shanks – have already arrived.

A Purple moorhen peers cautiously from among the reeds. The red patch above its bill and the adjacent purple glisten in the evening sun. Two red-wattled lapwings take off, loudly protesting against the intrusion. A Common kingfisher, a jewel on the wing, shoots its way just above the water, almost skimming the surface.

On my way back in the evening I saw flocks of birds returning to their roosts. A flock of Blossom-headed parakeets dashes across the already crimson sky, in formation flight, like an air force squadron. They dipped and banked before landing on their nightly roost. A bunch of bulbuls had gathered in a thicket for their night chatter.

Crossing the nullah and hurry to hit the road before nightfall, I heard the Shama again. An abundant feeling of gratitude flooded within me, for the birds, for Shama and for its song as I headed towards the teashop where the man was busy lighting his hurricane lamp.

–

The Hindu
(27.2.1977)

Cranes: Messengers From Heaven

What is the colour of snow like? It is like a white crane.

– Nirvana Sutra

Zen monk, nature writer and explorer Peter Matthiessen was in India in 2012 to observe the crane phenomenon at Kichan village in Rajasthan, where these graceful migrants – common and demoiselle cranes – gather by the thousands to feed on the grains strewn for them by the villagers. This is a community ritual that has been going on for the past 115 years. Matthiessen traveled on to Gujarat to watch sarus cranes in their home territory. It was part of his worldwide peregrination to observe all the cranes of the world. The result is a fascinating book *The Birds of Heaven: Travels with Cranes* (2003). Matthiessen points out that the plight of cranes all over the world has become a metaphor for vanishing wildlife.

Cranes are long-legged birds with long necks and bills. Though they look like large storks, they are very different. All cranes nest on the ground, while storks nest on treetops.

They are among the oldest of birds on earth; nine-million-year-old fossils of Sandhill cranes have been found in Wyoming. In India, we can see five species: The Common Crane, the Demoiselle, the Siberian, the Black-necked, and Sarus cranes. Only the last two are residents; the rest are winter visitors.

All the fifteen species of cranes, both in the Old and New worlds, are subjects of myths and legends in many cultures. Once regarded as messengers from heaven, but they are now threatened. Being sensitive to human interference and slow breeders makes the task of protecting them difficult. War, hunting, habitat destruction, and reclaiming wetlands have all taken their toll, and many of the crane species are doddering on the brink of extinction.

Hence, in 1973, the International Crane Foundation was formed in Wisconsin to protect these magnificent birds, many of which migrate to warmer climes thousands of kilometres away during winters. Matthiessen teamed up with five ornithologists and journeyed across the world, from New Mexico to Hokkaido in Japan and on to the outback in Australia. In this effort at creating awareness about the cranes, he was joined by local conservation enthusiasts, from Mongolian herdsmen to Australian aboriginals. He recorded this experience of travel, spread over ten years, in this memorable book. The exquisite paintings and drawings of the cranes by bird artist Robert Bateman add to the value of the book.

While writing about the fortunes of Siberian cranes, he refers to Richard Meinertzhagen, the notorious ornithologist. Recently, *The New York Times* published an article exposing a scientific fraud this British army officer had committed to gain ornithological fame. However, he, along with Salim Ali, first reported the sighting of Siberian crane in Bharatpur in 1937. He left a note that he and Salim Ali shot one of these cranes for the pot.

The Siberian crane has attracted notice for centuries. Ustad Mansur, the court painter of Jehangir, painted this bird. A. O. Hume saw them in Leh in 1854 and described them as 'the lily of birds'. As late as 1964, 200 cranes visited Bharatpur. For the last few years, none have been sighted. The Black-necked crane breeds in the marshy land and bogs of Ladakh. Its population has fallen steeply in the last few decades. Disturbance by tourists and predation of chicks by stray dogs are pointed out as reasons.

There is a distinction between nature writing and writing on wildlife. In the former, the writer responds to nature intuitively, in the manner of Thoreau. The writer on wildlife presents scientific findings in a readable manner. Matthiessen combines these two types of writing admirably. He built up an awesome reputation as a writer through works such as *The African Silence*, in which he wrote about his search for the pygmy elephants and the snow leopard with a gripping account of his trek, in the company of the legendary wildlifer George Schaller, along the Himalayas trying to get a glimpse of the elusive cat. "Lyrical" is the adjective often used to describe his writing.

The word pictures he created have the power of virtual reality. Here is a sample from *The Birds of Heaven*, in which he describes an incident while looking for the breeding grounds of the Siberian crane: "A steppe fox whisks through the blowing grass, a steppe eagle scoops on a young marmot. The eagle glares at the oncoming vehicles as it tears away red shining shreds. Neatly, then, it eviscerates the rodent, leaving the heavy guts behind as it takes wing, dragging the rest away over the grass."

Various conservation issues also come up for discussion in The Birds of Heaven. He writes about the problems in China, a country with an abysmal record of conservation, about tampering with rivers by building dams and about Lake Baikal in Russia which stores one-fifth of the world's fresh water. There are pen pictures of individuals who worked to save the cranes in various parts of the world. These include Prakash Jain, who renounced everything to work for cranes in Rajasthan and Finley Gilbert, an Australian aborigine, who provided information on the Brolga crane, a close relative of the Sarus. About his own motivation, Matthiessen records, "I care profoundly about cranes and tigers, not only as magnificent and stirring creatures, but as heralds and symbols of all that is being lost."

–

The Hindu
(27.05.2007)

Ballerina Of The Lake

Aged Banyan trees flank the road from Mysore to Heggadadevankotte, winding through rice fields and quaint little hamlets. Like many of the old Mysore roads, it frequently skirts picturesque lakes. In winter, these waterbodies are full and attract a host of resident and migratory waterfowl. There is one particular lake full of lotus blossoms which has been a favourite stop for us. My friend Sri Kantha, the bird photographer, had drawn our attention to this spot.

Sitting under the shade of a Banyan, we trained our binoculars on the far side of lake and Little grebes, Grey herons, godwits, coots and sandpipers resolved themselves into view. A spring of Common teals was resting at the water's edge. A lone raptor – Marsh harrier – came circling over the lake, looking for a meal and the grebes disappeared underwater quickly.

But the most colourful of all birds is the Pheasant-tailed Jacana; a pigeon sized bird of predominantly white, black and yellow plumage. It lives on the seeds of various aquatic plants and the small creatures found in water. This bird is adapted to walking over floating vegetation and marsh. So it is long legged, and long-toed to distribute its weight over a large area. You can see it run over the leaves, chasing a prey. At times when it spreads its wings in a flash of white, to balance, you are reminded of a ballerina. In Europe it is known as the Lily-trotter. When it steps on the floating leaf, it goes under water a bit and gives the illusion that the bird is walking on water. So in Papua New Guinea it is known as "Jesus Bird". For the Tamil villager, it is *Thamarai kozhi*, literally, the lotus fowl. If you pass by a lake with lotus and other floating vegetation in winter, stop and look for this bird.

A close cousin of this bird, but much less picturesque, the Bronze-winged Jacana is also sometimes seen alongside. Both the birds are oriented to an aquatic life. But the Pheasant-tailed Jacana is much more trusting and can be seen in ponds close to villages. I have seen them in small tanks right inside towns in Gujarat. Its call is a soft mew that could be mistaken for a cat in distress.

In winter, the Jacana is decked in its breeding plumage, sporting a sickle shaped tail that gives it the name. Its nest, made of weeds, almost floats in water. Birds have worked out many devices to protect their nests from predators and the Jacana has its floating nest. The peg-top shaped eggs are arranged in the nest with the small ends pointing inwards, to prevent them from rolling and falling out. Wildlife filmmaker Ashish Chandola had titled the beautiful film he made on this bird 'A Floating Home'. The female of this species is polyandrous and may lay more than one clutch of eggs. The respective males tend the other nests and carry out the chores of incubating and raising the young. This bird is extraordinary in other ways also. It carries its young in the folds of its wings as it moves over water.

Being warm-blooded creatures, birds' eggs need continuous warmth and so the bird has to incubate constantly. That is the reason why most of the nests are in the feeding area of the bird. Megapodes, of course, are an exception. They do not incubate but control the temperature by heaping leaf litter on top of their eggs.

Waterfowl such as the Jacana are symbols of the well-being of our environment, particularly wetlands. When you see birds in a lake, it is an indication that the water has not been polluted. But lakes and other waterbodies are disappearing fast. Ashish Kothari points out that of all the habitats it is the wetland that faces greatest danger. If they are near a city, the pressure to reclaim is great and insidiously, they disappear right in front of your eyes. In Chennai you can observe this vanishing process in Adyar estuary and Pallikarani marshes where we have spotted Jacanas. After a few years, only the name will remind you that there was once a waterbody there, such as the Lake Area in Chennai. In Coimbatore, much of Valangulam lake has been reclaimed. I have seen a Forest department note of the 1930s that Bar-headed geese were sighted in this lake. In Salem, a large lake has yielded place to the new Central bus-stand.

A waterbody is not merely a home to birds and other creatures; it is a resource for humans, providing water and fish. Described as 'waterlogged wealth' a wetland is a self-sustaining unit. Yet, we do not even have an idea of how many lakes and wetlands there are in the country. The WWF-India brought of The Directory of Wetlands in 1993, which listed about 170 spots that are important wildlife habitats. But there are thousands of others that are sustaining agriculture and recharge the water table. Our water shortage is directly connected with the disappearance of lakes. On the one hand, we reclaim, rather steal, the wetlands by dumping garbage and debris, and on the other hand, we propagate rain harvesting. It is a good example of being pound foolish and penny wise.

–

The Hindu
(16.02.2003)

Birding in the African Bush

Few sanctuaries in the world are known for their high density of bird life as the South Luangwa National park in Zambia. Five of us, all keen on birds, journeyed towards this destination. Early one morning, the ten-seater Beechcraft plane we were flying in, landed on the tiny Mfuwe airstrip. Thanks to the marvel of Internet, we knew that Andrew Phiri, our guide for the next six days and a birder himself, would be meeting us. We headed towards the wildlife camp 24 kilometres away, with Andrew at the wheel of the Land Rover, and a well-thumbed copy of Roberts's *Birds of Southern Africa* and a pair of binoculars by his side.

The Great Rift Valley in Africa, a large fissure on the face of Earth, is an awesome geological feature. This 4000 kilometre long valley begins in Ethiopia and goes up to Zambia. Some of the best wildlife habitats of the world, including alkaline lakes, hot springs and craters, are in this rift. Luangwa sanctuary is at the southern end of the valley. It is the river Luangwa, flowing through the area, that gives the national park its name. One of the largest sanctuaries in Africa, spread over 9000 square kilometres, it has enjoyed protection over a hundred years. The wealth of wildlife here came to the attention of the outside world when explorers like David Livingstone visited these areas in 1899.

Different types of vegetation provide varied habitats to a large concentration of life forms. The semi-deciduous Miombo type of forest predominates. It is not dense, so viewing is easy. Vast areas are scrubland with tall trees. There are stretches of savannah and there is the river, flanked by the riverine forest. Now and then a great baobab tree makes its appearance.

As you set out during daybreak, an orchestra of bird calls surrounds you. Birds that are familiar to you through the field guides make their appearance. The first to show up during our visit was the Saddle-billed stork, a colourful bird, sedately walking in a shallow pond.

One can see quite a few varieties of hornbills, the most spectacular of them being the Ground hornbill. Bee-eaters, of which there are more than five species here, seem to be constantly in view. They catch their prey in midair, demonstrating their aerial prowess. These colourful birds are a delight to watch and the most colourful of them is the Carmine bee-eater which migrates into this area in August. But a few vanguard flocks seemed to have arrived and we were able to spot them more than once.

Our guide, Andrew, turned out to be another resourceful dimension of the trip. He knew his birds. Even as a bird flitted from bush to bush, he would identify it. From its call, he would tell us whether it was a male or female Fishing Eagle. When we expressed a desire to see Crested cranes, for which this sanctuary is well known, he took us one bitterly cold morning to a savannah area 50 kilometres away. Not only did we see the cranes; we also visited a hot spring, a geological remnant of the volcanic past.

Cranes, of which there are fifteen species, is one of the oldest of birds on Earth; nine-million-year-old fossils of Sandhill cranes have been found in Wyoming. Andrew told us that birders came here just to spot a specific bird, often the Pel's Fishing Owl. We were fortunate to spot it by ourselves while on a cruise in the river Zambezi.

Occasionally a species you have seen in India appears and surprises you. The Pied King fisher is one such. And there are birds that appear similar to those back home, but turn out to be a different species. Such is the Yellow-billed stork, which looks remarkably like the Painted stork of our countryside. We visited an enormous breeding colony of these birds on two large trees. Beneath the trees were scores of Marabou storks, patiently waiting for the pieces of fish that fell while the nestlings were being fed by the parents.

One bird that catches one's attention in East Africa is the Hammerkop, so called because of its hammer-shaped head. The names of many African birds carry a Dutch flavour, thanks to the Afrikaans language. This brown-plumaged, egret-like bird builds enormous nests in the branches of trees not far from water. It belongs to a unique family of its own. Another bird characteristic of Southern Africa is the Ox pecker, which comes in two varieties. You see them perched on giraffes and zebras, feeding on the ticks. While returning from the safari one night, a herd of buffalos crossed the road; in the light of our headlamps, we could see Ox peckers hanging on to them, even in that darkness.

My most enduring image of my birding days in the bush was the iconic African Fishing eagle cruising over Luangwa River, its plaintive call resonating over the valley. One day we were sitting by the river – our camp was on the bank – and were able to watch this majestic raptor swoop down and grab a fish in its talons in an amazing display of aerodynamics.

–

The Hindu

(24.08.2008)

A Colourful Sentry

In that rest house on the banks of Kaveri, it was siesta time. The silence of the afternoon was pierced by bell-like, fluid calls of a Bee-eater, floating by from a distance. Not their usual chatter, but even notes uttered at regular intervals. My young friend Sri Kantha, cleaning his photographic gear, had also noticed the call and joined me as I set out to investigate.

We walked along the river. Not far, a small canal joined the river. On the far side bank of the dry canal we could spot a lone Bee-eater, sitting on the edge and calling. On seeing us approach, the bird flew off, silently. As soon as it took to wing, we saw another Bee-eater emerge from a hole in the soil above the dry bed of canal. We had located a nesting pair! A small jamun tree nearby, in spite of its mutilated crown, provided adequate shade; we squatted and began a vigil, I, with my binoculars, and Sri Kantha with his camera. In the clear blue sky above, four Open-billed storks had found a thermal and were spiraling up, Icarus-like, on motionless wings to an unknown destination. On land, an unseen Cicada provided a droning background with it shrill noise.

The Small Green Bee-eater, the very species that caught our attention that afternoon in Srirangapatna, is the smallest of the five varieties of Bee-eaters found in India. The most colourful is the Chestnut-headed Bee-eater, which is spotted on hillsides. However, the most picturesque of all Bee-eaters in the world is the crimson plumaged Carmine Bee-eater on which I had set my eyes but once; in a bare, dark thorny tree in Masai Mara, Kenya, I had seen them flitting like little flames of fire. Bee-eaters are birds of the Old World; you do not see them in the Americas.

Our Bee-eaters, the subject of our story, were earlier known as Common Bee-eaters. These green little birds can be seen in the countryside on fences overhead cables from where they periodically sally forth and catch an insect in midair, come back to their perch, batter the prey to death and swallow it. They often gather in hundreds while roosting for the night.

The horizontal hole on the bank of the canal, from which the Bee-eater had emerged, was the entrance to a tunnel which would end in a widened egg chamber. Both the female and male would have excavated that warren; now both were busy feeding the nestlings inside. There is no way to distinguish male from female; both look alike.

In the amoral world of birds, there are two types of monogamy. One type, to which the Bee-eater belongs, lasts just for a breeding season; the male shares all parental chores and remains with its mate till the nest is empty. In the other, the birds mate for life, like the Sarus crane.

Once a parent is inside the tunnel, it is extremely vulnerable. So the Bee-eaters have worked out a foolproof security system to facilitate feeding the nestlings. When one bird goes into the tunnel with food for the nestling, the other sits close to the entrance and keeps up this distinct call which seem to tell the bird inside that everything alright outside. In the face of any intrusion, the sentry flies away; once the call stops, the bird inside senses danger and rushes out. They both return when the threat is passed.

For a bird photographer – Sri Kantha is one – sighting a nesting bird is a consummation devoutly to be wished for. The bird will have a fixed perch or two near the nest. As the photographer fixes his focus on this perch and waits, the bird comes into the frame and the picture is in the bag. My friend had mounted a 500 mm telephoto lens (pre-digital days) and was shooting without a tripod. I recalled being with M. Krishnan in Anamalai Sanctuary when he encountered a camera-wielding wildlifer. "Is that a 400 mm on your camera? And you are shooting handheld?" asked Krishnan, in a tone of surprise and after a moment added, "Brave man". Sri Kantha, however, assured me that the tele lenses of today could be comfortably handheld and used. He was to demonstrate that convincingly with his pictures of the Bee-eaters.

The birds kept up a steady supply of food, mostly winged insects – bees, dragonflies and wasps – and provided many photo opportunities. Not satisfied, Sri Kantha whipped out his Swiss knife and cut a crooked branch from an oleander bush nearby. He sharpened one end, walked across the canal, and drove the branch into earth close to the hole, providing a perch that the birds could not miss and gave a good angle for his camera. It took only an hour for the birds to accept this new addition to the environment and my friend got many good shots. The bird, as if to reward his patience, flew in with a Red dragonfly and for a split second, even presented its profile.

–

The Hindu
(01.09.2002)

The Grebes Of Dwaraka

If you want to observe the dramatic spectacle of bird migration, there are few arenas in India that can rival Gujarat, particularly the western part of the state. One explanation is that this area is smack on one of the major flyways of . The large number of lakes and marshes that dot the countryside, the Great Rann of Kutch, parts of which gets inundated after the monsoon, the vast mud flats of the Gulfs of Kutch and Cambay, and the long coastline, are features that attract the migrants. Added to this is the abiding Gujarati tradition of not harming birds. Nearly 14% of waterfowl migrating to India, spend the winter in Gujarat. In the beginning of the migratory season, September and October, we could observe these birds quite easily and from much closer quarters, closer than in any other location that I have experienced. A journey across the Gujarat countryside in winter can hold many surprises for a birdwatcher.

Four of us, all committed twitchers, left Jamnagar early one October morning and headed towards Bhet Dwaraka, to sight Oystercatchers that congregate there in the mud flats. About thirty kilometres before our destination, we passed through a vast stretch of salt pans. The impounded water had attracted a bewildering variety of birds: pelicans, gulls, flamingos, terns, herons and egrets.

The birds of passage and the residents mingled in one joyous, noisy concourse.

Among these, a flock of black and brown plumaged birds swimming in a pond by the roadside caught our eyes. One look and I knew it was a 'lifer' for me, a bird that one sees for the first time in one's life. The flock was touchingly trusting, and we could observe it from close quarters. The birds were buoyant, sitting so lightly on the water surface and nonchalantly riding the small waves created by the chill wind that blew across the bare landscape. Their soft, short monosyllable whistling calls came floating by. By the shape of their dumpy, tailless body and the slightly upturned beak, we could identify them as grebes. But which variety? The coral red eyes and their size, that of a pigeon, revealed them as Black-necked Grebes, rare visitors seen only in North Western India during winter. They have been sighted in the lakes of Ladakh also. Its home range is Western Europe; when the waterbodies there start freezing in winter, these birds head south to warmer climes. Of the four varieties seen in India, only the Black-necked grebe is gregarious.

The most common grebe seen all over India is the Little Grebe, the smallest aquatic bird of India. This tiny tailless bird dives under water with lightning speed when alarmed. Salim Ali says that this bird's reflexes are so quick that when shot at, it would dive underwater before the charge could reach it. Grebes are aquatic diving birds, with short wings and almost no tail. The largest grebe in India is the Crested Grebe, known for its spectacular courtship movements. I have seen that display only once, in Barapani near Shillong. Though I visited many wetlands in Gujarat looking for birds, I never saw the Black-necked grebe anywhere again.

It is a birder's experience that he sees some birds only once in a lifetime. The Black-necked Grebe was one such rare sighting. Another bird I have sighted only on one occasion is the Peacock pheasant. Driving to Mawsynram, the wettest place on earth, in

Meghalaya one evening I negotiated a hairpin bend and there they were, by the edge of the road: a pair of Peacock pheasants. As they scurried into the underbrush, the iridescent green spots on their plumage glistened in the mellowed rays of the evening sun.

While returning from Bhet Dwaraka, we stopped when we spotted a dead Grey pelican at the same place beneath high-tension wires; presumably it had been electrocuted. We noticed that one of its legs bore a ring with a number and code. The Bombay Natural History Society, to whom one in our group sent the ring, identified it as having been ringed in Kazakhstan.

–

The Hindu
(02.08.1995)

Birds Of An Island

In his book, *Song of the Dodo*, biologist David Quammen talks about creatures of oceanic islands and how geographical isolation triggers speciation. The dodo of Mauritius is the best-known example of this kind of development. In that Indian Ocean island, with no predator to worry about, the dodo, a turkey-sized flightless bird, flourished for millennia till humans landed there in the 18th century. However, Quammen points out that geographical isolation does not always result in appearance of new species. But when new species evolve, they do so only in isolation. Of all the life forms, it is this bird species that reflect this feature noticeably. It was the finches of Galapagos Island that led Charles Darwin to his theory of evolution. This was brought home to us dramatically when we spent a few days in one of the islands in the Andaman Nicobar archipelago in 2000.

Havelock Island is about two hours by boat from Port Blair. Surrounded by emerald-hued lagoons, much of the mountainous island is covered with tropical evergreen forests. In some stretches, mangrove swamps line the island shores. Settlers live in the coastal area. We stayed at a resort in the shadow of the forest, in thatched cottages standing on stilts on the pattern of Nicobaric huts. Within walkable distance was a cove, fringed by immensely tall trees. Bird calls were constantly in the air. It was a landscape of primeval splendour.

On the first day, while wading in the crystal-clear waters of the lagoon, I saw two birds land on a mangrove tree to my right. One look and I knew this was a lifer for me, a bird species you see for the first time in your life. They were White-headed mynas. Within minutes, a woodpecker with a white-barred black mantle and red crown, landed on the same tree and started pecking at the bark, feeding on unseen grub. Another lifer: This was a Fulvous-breasted woodpecker! Both these birds are exclusive to the Andamans.

The 324 islands of the Andaman Nicobar archipelago are in fact the tops of a submerged mountain chain which is a continuation of the Arakan Yoma of Myanmar. But they have been separated from the mainland long enough to have developed avifauna of their own. These islands are home to about 242 bird species, of which 39 are unique to the islands. Ornithologists describe them as endemic, meaning birds that have evolved into distinctive species because of the insularity of their habitats. The birds are quite trusting, and it is easy to observe them. Soon we were able to see more endemic species, including the Olive-backed sunbird and Andaman Swallow. These islands are the proverbial paradise for birdwatchers.

After the 1857 Rising, the British government turned its attention to the Andaman Islands to explore the possibility of setting up a penal colony. Following that development, a few amateur ornithologists from the British civil services visited the islands and collected bird specimens. It was a period in which collecting eggs, nests and bird pelts was a consuming passion among some of the officers.

Among the collectors was A. O. Hume, better known as the founder of the Indian National Congress. He made a few visits and collected specimens. Based on these collections, he wrote a series of articles between 1874 and 1876 in *Stray Feathers*, a journal of natural history that he edited. At least one bird in the Andamans is named after Hume – the White collared Kingfisher

(*Todiramphus chloris humii*) – and it is easily spotted in the jetty area of Port Blair.

It was Hume who first got a specimen of the Narcondam hornbill, one of the well-known endemic birds of this archipelago. The entire population of these of these colourful hornbills, about 300, is confined to a single forested island Narcondam, about five square kilometres in area. Another endemic bird one can easily spot in Port Blair itself is the Andaman Crow pheasant.

After taxonomist Humayun Abdul Ali of the Bombay Natural History Society carried out a series of surveys in the nineteen eighties and published his observations, the unrivalled nature of the bird fauna of the islands became clear to ornithologists across the world. The megapode, a bird the size of a hen, which has come to symbolize the endemic birds of Andamans, inhabits the Nicobar Islands. It lays its eggs on the ground and covers it with sand and dried leaves. The precocious chicks hatch out and fend for themselves. Another distinct bird is the Nicobar pigeon, unmistakable with its metallic green hackles and sheen on its plumage.

During the last three days of our holidays, we stayed in the cottages of ANET (Andaman Nicobar Ecology Team) located in a forest in Wandoor. Every morning at daybreak – which is 4.30 am here – we would hear hauntingly long-drawn, fluid bird calls. Peeping through the window we could see a Shama singing and pirouetting in a bamboo clump. The plumage was a little different from the Shama we had seen in the mainland. A quick look at the book revealed that this was indeed a sub-species, exclusive to the Andamans: the White-rumped Shama (*Copsychus malabaricus albiventris)*. Arguably the best songbird in the world, Shama is a forest dweller and difficult to spot. For a birder, the sight of this bird announcing the arrival of a new day is a great blessing.

–

The Hindu
(02.10.2005)

A Harbinger Of Monsoon

When we lived in Vellore, we had a neighbour who had an unusual manner of greeting: "Do you think it will rain today?" So we had nicknamed him *Sathaka paravai*. The story is that this Sathaka bird keeps flying all the time, never perching anywhere and survives by drinking only rainwater. So the bird is always longing for rain, like my neighbour. This is just one of the mythical birds, like *Annam* (swan) of Tamil literature, which is credited with the ability to separate milk and water.

However, there is a bird associated with the monsoon, and its Hindi name is *Chatak* (Pied Crested Cuckoo). Its appearance in South India just before the monsoon heralds the arrival of rain. A bird the size of a myna, it is predominantly black, with white abdomen and white wing patches. The long tail has white tips. The prominent crests gives its Tamil name *Kondai kuyil.* Around September, you begin to hear its plaintive calls, particularly during the hot part of the day. When these characteristically cuckoo-like fluid calls "pee-pee pew" come floating in the air, it means that rains are on their way.

I have often heard and seen them in Mogappair area in Chennai around open spaces. Sometimes you see them perched on overhead cables. Feeding on caterpillars and other insects, it is a typical cuckoo in its breeding habits, laying its eggs in the nest of Common babblers. To facilitate this parasitism, the eggs of this cuckoo closely resemble those the babblers, being bright turquoise blue. After they hatch out, the nestling cuckoos push the chicks of the foster parents out of the nest so that they can garner all the food. In the amoral world of birds, the imperative is to breed successfully. There is one Indian cuckoo, however, which builds its own nest – the Crow-pheasant – a common bird of our countryside.

Another cuckoo, a close relative of our Pied crested cuckoo, makes an occasional appearance in this part of the country. It is the Red-winged crested cuckoo, slightly larger, more colourful, and seeks wooded areas. With its red wings and black body, it is easily spotted. It breeds in North East India and migrates south. In the early nineteen seventies, enthused by the initial waves of conservation efforts, a group of us set out to prepare a checklist of birds of the Guindy Deer park.

My friend and fellow twitcher "10-volume Narayanaswamy" recorded the presence of this cuckoo in Guindy and surprised even a seasoned birder like M. Krishnan. You might wonder about the prefix to his name. When other birders barely managed to possess a copy of Salim Ali's *Book of Indian Birds*, Narayanaswamy was the proud owner of the all the 10 volumes of the newly released *Handbook of the Birds of India and Pakistan* by Salim Ali and Dillon Ripley. Hence his identity.

Hopefully, these two birds would continue to show up and enliven the southern countryside with their calls. Birds are the most visible indicators of the well-being of our environment and our biodiversity heritage.

–

The Hindu

The Storks Of Koondhankulam

In quite few places in India, Painted storks, stately and colourful birds of the plains, nest in villages with the protection of the locals. In Gujarat, you can see breeding colonies inside towns such as Bhavnagar and Baruch. The village of Koondhankulam near Tirunelveli in Tamil Nadu is another such site where Painted storks, known to the villagers as *Sanguvalai narai*, raise their young amongst human habitation.

For many years, this village of nine thousand people, mostly agriculturists, Pannaiyars, has been the breeding centre for these storks. Trustingly, they nest in the trees that dot the village, in the backyards and by the roadside, at times even in the low-slung Prosopis trees. The villagers, vegetarians all, have guarded the birds zealously. If anyone was caught killing a bird, they would tie the dead bird around his neck and parade him through the village. Years ago, Painted storks used to nest in tamarind trees in Moondradaipu village on the main Tirunelveli-Nagercoil highway. With the increase in vehicular traffic and harassment, those birds have abandoned that spot and presumably they have also moved in here.

The arrival of the storks in large numbers is an indication that the rains have been good and that there would be enough water for two crops. Unmindful of the stench and cacophony, the villagers welcome these birds as they indicate good times to come. The storks arrive by the end of the monsoon, in January, and stay on till June.

But what is special about Koondhankulam is that at the edge of the village, in the safety of *Acacia nilotica* trees on a lakeside, hundreds of Grey pelicans, spoonbills and darters nest. It is this lake which gives its name to this village. (*Kulam* in Tamil means a lake. In Tirunelveli district there are many places with names end with the term *kulam*.) All these three species are in the endangered list, and if they breed successfully in a site, they have to be given all possible protection. These Acacia trees have been raised here under social forestry scheme and now provide a venue for a breeding colony. In 1993, steps were afoot to auction these trees as fuel wood. That is when the villagers got together, and through their panchayat, persuaded the Forest Department to spare the trees. The very next year, this place was declared a sanctuary and a committee formed at the village to ensure the birds' safety.

Waterfowl gather in large numbers during the breeding season and nest in colonies in spots where food is plentiful and there is security, like Koondhankulam. These sites, heronries as they are called, serve as an indicator of the status of wetlands in the country. Critical to the environment, wetlands maintain subterranean water, sustains food chains, control floods and provide habitat for wildlife. The 129-hectare Koondhankulam lake, which receives water from Manimuthar canal, lies on the western side of the village. This lake and the neighbouring water bodies such as Kadankulam, Ilamalkulam, Sungulam and Vijayanarayanan lake, brimming with fish and other small aquatic life after the monsoon, serve as feeding grounds for the waterfowl. Pate, a former Collector of Tirunelveli, has recorded in the District Gazetteer, published in 1914, that pelicans regularly fed in Vijayanarayanan lake.

In the countryside around Koondhankulam, a large number of other species of birds are also seen. Evidently, this area has not been polluted by pesticides. I saw Brahminy kites soaring above the lake and a Montague's harrier flying low, examining the edge of water for possible prey. Black ibis, along with Cattle egret, were feeding in a field being ploughed. There were rollers enlivening the countryside with their brilliant colours.

It is crucial that the heronry here is left undisturbed. Buses and vans should not be allowed to come into the village. Currently, they pass just a few feet from the nests. When we were at the lake, a van came right up to the bund. If this is not stopped now, we will have a situation like Vedanthangal sanctuary, where at any given time dozens of vehicles are parked by the lake. A sanctuary is primarily for birds; tourism can only be incidental.

The story will be incomplete if I do not write about Paul Pandi, part-time forest watcher. When I trained my binoculars on a dabchick, he whispered in my ear that this tiny bird swims with its chick on its back, piggyback style. He pointed to a Glossy ibis, a shiny black wader perched on a palmyrah tree, as the *anril* bird of Tamil classics that pairs for life. He was right on both counts. His fascination with birds does not stop with mere knowledge. He rescues the nestlings that fall from trees, hand rears and releases them. Every season, his orphanage has at least four or five pelicans and an equal number of storks. If systematic ringing were done for these young ones before they are released into the wild, it would be easier to follow them. In the heronry at Kokrebelur near Mysore, volunteers hand rear pelican fledglings that fall from nests, then colour band them for easy identification.

We should remember that all the birds that nest in Koondhankulam, as elsewhere, are local birds, not migratory. A bird is a resident of the place where it nests. The migratory birds, such as stilts, sandpipers and godwits, can also be sighted here, but they are winter visitors and come to Koondhankulam and other lakes only to feed. I saw migratory ducks of many varieties in vast numbers. There were Pintails, Mallards and Blue-winged teals. Our own resident duck, the Spot bill, was also there in large numbers along with Comb-ducks.

The celebrity among this lake's winter visitors is certainly the Bar-headed goose. These birds breed in Ladakh and come south in winter. This is the southernmost point where they can be seen. There is no record of their being sighted in Sri Lanka. That morning, we saw skein after skein of these geese arrive at the lake, after overnight feeding in the fields around. Their honking calls as they came through the morning mist and dropped wings to land, charged the landscape with a magical quality.

–

The Hindu
(17.12.2006)

The Return Of The Pelican

Early one morning, driving across Muttukadu bridge on our way to Mamallapuram, on our right we noticed what looked like a large white flotsam in the lagoon. Through the binoculars it resolved into a flock of pelicans indulging in communal feeding. These birds form a sort of flotilla, drive the fish with the heavy beats of their wings to shallower waters and then scoop them in their beaks which function as their landing nets.

Thanks to the Internet, many birders have been informing fellow twitchers of the frequent sightings of pelicans in recent months, in and around Chennai. Dr. Shantharam recorded having seen nearly two hundred of these birds sitting on a pylon in Pallikaranai. Once a rare visitor to Vedanthangal, pelicans are now nesting there in the hundreds. Birdwatchers from around Bengaluru and Mysore have filed similar reports about pelican sightings. Good news.

A large water bird, the size of a turkey, the pelican is a bird with a long neck and a huge bill. An extendable gular pouch attached to this bill made Ogden Nash write his famous limerick on the bird and its unmistakable beak. Here it is:

A wonderful bird is the pelican
His bill can hold as much as his belly can
He can store in his beak

Enough food for a week
I don't how the hellican.

The Grey is found in lakes and lagoons. Its short legs and squat body has earned it its Tamil name Koozhaikada. It has come to symbolize our wetland habitats.

In addition to Vedanthangal, there are a number of spots where pelicans breed in this part of the country. At Kokrebelur near Mysore, their annual breeding spectacle attracts many visitors. In Nelapattu and Uppalapadu in Andhra, plenty of pelicans arrive every season for multiplying. Nelapattu, just 95 kilometres from Chennai, offers the best facility to observe their nesting activity. The barringtonia trees are not far from the watch-tower and you get a ringside view, including unobstructed sight of some nests. The nests are placed close to each other and the adult pelicans jostle with each other. The nest itself is quite skimpy, an elementary platform made of sticks and twigs. But the pelicans are hard sitters, with both the male and female sharing the brooding duty. Koonthankulam, near Tirunelveli, is a refuge where they nest annually. There are at least fifteen sites in Tamil Nadu where these birds breed annually. Pelicans need undisturbed places to reproduce and abandon their nests even at slight provocation.

While breeding, pelicans need a lot of food. To raise three or four ravenous nestlings exclusively on fish is no mean job. The adult bird swallows the fish and on reaching its nest, regurgitates half-digested fish to the nestlings In 2001 the forest department stocked the Vedanthangal Lake with nearly 50,000 fingerlings to help the nesting birds.

Some birders have raised a question whether sighting these birds in a few places could indicate recovery. Bengaluru-based ornithologist Dr. Subramanya, who has been meticulously documenting pelicanries all over India for nearly two decades, says that these sightings indeed augur well for the status of this magnificent bird. We have reasons to believe that pelicans, symbolizing our wetland habitats, are making a comeback. He points out that the increase in pelican numbers in South India is also due to the large number of breeding sites where raising *Acacia nilotica* has provided places to nest. A decade ago, the sighting of this bird was a rare occurrence. For instance, in 1991, only thirteen birds were seen around Bengaluru. Now you see them almost the year around; once a birder saw a flock of 240 in a single tank on a single day.

However, the overall picture of waterfowl is not so bright. The Wetland International, an outfit monitoring the status of waterfowl the world over, says that 62% of water birds in Asia are on the decline, the main reason being habitat destruction. Veteran birder Lavkumar Kachar from Ahmedabad laments that the majestic Sarus crane (the Krauncha bird of *Ramayana*) is on its way out.

–

The Hindu
(18.02.2007)

Beneath The Canopy

A patch of rain forest is in the Indira Gandhi National park in the Western Ghats in Coimbatore District. We were at the periphery of the forest, waiting for our guide, Natarajan. As a birder, this forester has built up a formidable reputation. To be able to go birding with him would be a dream come true for any bird enthusiast. If the locale is a tropical rain forest that would be the ultimate treat.

The Suruli tree beneath which we were standing was a scene of much activity. We spotted small minivets, Yellow bulbuls and even a pair of Ruby-throated bulbuls. At this point, we noticed Natarajan, neatly turned out in his uniform, walking briskly towards us with a machete in his hand.

He led us single file along a bridle path into the patch of rain forest, known as *Karian shola*. Once he was with us, our bird list soared. He has this uncanny ability to spot even those birds that were cryptically camouflaged, almost as though the birds sent him ESP signals of their presence. He drew our attention to an Orange-headed ground thrush under a bush just a few feet away, deftly turning over dead leaves looking for insects. A tiny bird that flitted in and out of a scrub was a Spider hunter. It was here that Natarajan casually asked if we would like to see Ceylon frogmouth. This nocturnal bird is so protectively coloured that is almost impossible to spot it in the forest and none of us had seen this bird. Leaving us on the bridle path, he disappeared into the dense jungle.

The tropical rain forest, found in warm and high rainfall areas between the tropics of Cancer and Capricorn around the globe, is home to myriad life forms. A showcase for biodiversity, the sheer variety here is much greater than any in other terrestrial ecosystem. Both plants and animals form an intricately symbiotic web. This diversity is disappearing fast as rain forests are destroyed all over the world. Some of the rain forests of India, which is part of the Indo-Malayan chain, are in the Western Ghats.

The Ceylon frogmouth, a resident of the rain forest, evolved over eons to fit perfectly into that little ecological niche in the dark, moist habitat. Nocturnal and insectivorous, this myna-sized bird is so obliteratively plumaged that it can escape all but the trained eye. At day, it settles on a branch upright and sleeps with its beak pointing up, mimicking a dry stump. Its protective colouration ensures its safety. The bird gets its name from the wide, bristled mouth and large bill. At night it feeds on small insects, living on the ground and in tree branches. A close relative of the nightjar, it belongs to the family of frogmouths found mostly in Australia.

In fact, South India is the western-most point where members of this family can be seen. The Ceylon frogmouth builds its nest on horizontal branches, lines it with its own down feathers and lichen and lays a single egg. Both male and female share incubation duty. The bird is rare, and it was only in 1998 three years ago that this bird was reported from Anamalai sanctuary.

Natarajan returned silently like a ghost and motioned us to follow him; we walked behind him, single file. Within minutes we realized that leeches had climbed up our legs, in spite of shoes and socks. Periodically de-leeching and lopping off bushes to make way slowed our progress. A Green whipsnake on a bush provided photo opportunities. A raucous call from the canopy announced the presence of a Black woodpecker.

Natarajan slowed down, froze and pointed out to a clump of bamboo ahead. We peered for a few minutes but could not discern anything. Then suddenly, like an image on a hologram resolving itself, we could see three birds, a male, a young one and a female, huddled together on a stump at eye level, like a wood carving. This incredible concealment and deception is what saves the bird from roving predators as it sleeps defenceless. We remained there for nearly ten minutes. Through the binoculars, we could see that they were awake and watching us with their yellow eyes.

We came out of the forest, approached the wayside tea shop, and drank steaming hot tea from stainless-steel glasses while reviewing the events of the day. A leopard that struck fear in the neighbouring Sarkarpathi village had been tranquillized and released in that forest, a major operation for the forest staff that day. We had seen the rare Travancore tortoise, another denizen of the rain forests in the Western Ghats. But the enduring image will be that little family of birds, huddled together in their fast-shrinking habitat, one of the last few patches of rain forests left on earth.

–

The Hindu
(07.03.1999)

A Morning with the Raptors

A birdwatcher may sight some birds only once in a lifetime. I have seen the Brown fish owl only once, in Someswara wildlife sanctuary near Mangalore. Fortunately, I was able to set my eyes again on this magnificent bird in 2001.

We were driving through Bandipur National park early one morning. Our driver, a youngster with an alert peripheral vision and a good sense of birds, slowed down and whispered "owl" pointing to our right. There, on a low tree branch was this enormous, dumpy owl. When we trained our binoculars on it, the white bib and yellow eyes suggested its identity. We had adequate time to watch and take photographs before it took off. As it left its perch, we could see its legs clearly. They were bare and yellow, confirming that it was indeed the Brown Fish owl we had suspected. The other owl of similar size is the Great Horned owl, a denizen of dry country, and with legs covered with feathers. The Fish owl's legs, on the other hand, are designed without any feathers, so it can dip its feet into water to grab fish, in the manner of an Osprey. And unlike its cousin, the Fish owl can be active in mornings and evenings also.

Owls, unfortunately, are traditionally stigmatized in India. This may be because they are nocturnal and also because the owl we town dwellers are most likely to come across is the Barn owl, which has a blood curdling call. They often live right among human habitation. A few months ago, a Barn owl took residence in a house in Besant Nagar and we could watch it from the next house where my friend, a fellow birder, lives. He did not tell the neighbour about her new tenant, fearing she might decide to chase it away. A barn owl being mobbed by crows in the mornings is not an unusual sight in cities. This phenomenon, the encounter between owl and crow, is mentioned in *Thirukural*, the ancient Tamil work of couplets:

> A crow will conquer owl in broad daylight;
> The king that foes would crush, needs fitting time to fight.
>
> (481, G. U. Pope's translation)

My wife collects owl figurines of all media: ceramic, terracotta, glass and wood; we have a large silk screen print of four owls framed and hung in our home. Visitors ask us if the owl is not bad omen. Owl is in fact the mount of Lakshmi. When she is featured alone, it is the much-maligned owl that is her vahana. When she is with Vishnu, then of course she also rides along on Garuda, another raptor.

These nocturnal raptors are facing a grim future. A study of the WWF-India and TRAFFIC, the wildlife Trade Monitoring network, revealed that a large number of owls are caught and slaughtered for ritual purposes all over the country, particularly in Bihar and Uttar Pradesh. They are used in black magic rituals in which owl parts are used or the birds are sacrificed. The favoured day for these rituals is the New moon day. It is believed that tantriks can kill an owl, take its spirit off and put it in an amulet. In fact, there are books on how to conduct these rituals. Owl body parts, such as feathers and claws, are also used in folk medicine. The study suggests that due to the clampdown on trade in pet birds such as parrots, bird trappers have turned their attention to owls. Of the thirty species recorded in India, at least thirteen are being caught and sold. A barn owl can fetch as much as Rs. 3000.

Before the drive ended that morning, we were able to see two more raptors. On a dried branch, against the grey blue sky, was a Crested hawk eagle. When it is keyed up, the few long feathers on its head stand erect. As we watched this eagle, those feathers on the head were fluttering like little flags. Coming out of the sanctuary and joining the main road, we spotted a Pallid Harrier in the middle of the road, picking up some remnant of a roadkill. A lizard? We stopped the jeep, shut off the engine and had a close and clear look at this graceful migrant.

–

The Hindu
(18.11.2007)

The Birds Are Back

One feature that strikes a bird enthusiast returning to the United States after a break of a few years is the increasing presence of birds all around, even in big cities. There are diverse reasons for this: one is the heightened awareness of environmental protection. The other is that birds have been recognized as the most prominent indicators of the wellbeing of our environment and are cared for. But the crucial reason seems to be discontinuing the use of DDT. This deadly pesticide had proved harmful to birds into whose bodies it found its way through the small life in the field that form the prey base for most birds. DDT proved particularly lethal to raptors. Peregrine falcons nesting in the bridges of New York City and the triumphant return of the Bald eagle, once teetering on extinction, are parts of this success story.

On my first morning in New Orleans, we sat down for breakfast in the small garden laid in the back of my host's new house. To entice the birds, my friend had put up three different bird feeders: one with nectar, another with small seeds and the third with large seeds. These contraptions ensured a stream of visitors. Before we finished eating, we had seen a Red throated hummingbird, a cardinal, a jay, a Red-headed woodpecker and a Red-winged black bird. Add to this a Red-tailed hawk that flew over. All through, two squirrels waited on the ground to pick the nuts that dropped from the feeders as the birds fed.

The tremendous enthusiasm for birdwatching is a big factor in getting birds protected. One out of four in America is a bird-enthusiast. On any day, you see small groups of keen birders scouring the bushes in Central Park in New York. Birdwatching is considered one of the fast spreading hobbies. When a person takes to birdwatching, soon her concerns widen to cover conservation issues and eventually to larger environmental concerns. Many wildlifers and environmentalists in India also started as birdwatchers and followed this trajectory.

Bird counts, like the Asian Winter Waterfowl count we do in India, are done directly online. Each birder puts in his observation directly into the Internet. In a few days, the latest figures are available for everyone. Similarly, rare sightings are reported online. In fact, for mobilizing support for conservation causes and for activism related to environment, Internet is being used in a big way. In India, this practice is just beginning, thanks to individuals like Ashish Pittie of Hyderabad and R.Shantharam of Chennai. Institutional use of Internet for conservation purposes is yet to catch on. Yahoo groups of birders have been formed and each sighting is recorded. Migrant Watch is another group which documents online the occurrence of migrants all over the country.

The groundswell of support for conservation in the United States is the result of many events organized by conservation groups. The Bird marathon is one such. For the past 18 years, the Audubon Society at New Jersey has been organizing a competition among birdwatchers every summer to spot as many birds as they can in a span of 24 hours. The event, called World Series of Birding, was on in May and I closely followed it. Birders from all over the country come in to participate in this bird marathon. A team should consist of a minimum of two birders and the contest begins at midnight. The interesting point is that hearing a bird that is enough to log it. This enables the birder to record the presence of nocturnal birds. Secondly, the call of a bird is a much more reliable indication of its identity than its appearance. Therefore identification through calls is a more reliable method. This year, in 2012 the winning team in New Jersey competition logged 214 species.

In an afternoon walk around a small lake in Bronxville, a New York suburb, we sighted a number of birds. Large cormorants, blackbirds and mockingbirds. A night heron was fishing in daytime, breaking the rules of bird behaviour. Canada geese were all over; migrants from Canada, many of them have stayed on and started breeding in their domicile. They have proliferated so much that in some places they are a nuisance and gardens have what is known as a 'goose fence'. In this lake we saw a group of goslings feeding supervised by two geese. Were they male and female or were they two broods supervised by two females? We checked with a local birdwatcher who confirmed that they were indeed male and female. "They are sharing parental chores," he said and added with an impish smile, "Being politically correct."

–

The Hindu
(02.09.2001)

Where Black Swans Congregate

We were standing on the sandbar separating the Pacific Ocean and Lake Wollumboola. The sky was a clear cerulean blue and in front of us spread a spectacular sight, of thousands upon thousands of Black swans, along with myriads of other smaller waterfowl in the lagoon. On the far side, a forest of tall gum trees stood up to the water's edge. It was a primordial sight, without any indication of modern civilization. This is part of Jervis National Park, about 200 kilometres from Sydney

Aeons ago, during the Ice Age, the sea level rose due to glaciers melting and water spilled over into the land. Over the years, a wind-swept sand bar between the sea and the lake was formed, and a coastal lagoon came into being.

This brackish water lake offers food in the form of water plants and small aquatic lives, to sustain millions of waterfowl. Some birds, like the Little tern, nest here. The other birds seen here in great numbers are Chestnut teal, Grey teal and Little pied cormorant. For birdwatchers from India, some familiar species seen here include the Coot and the Oyster catcher. This lake is on the East Asia-Australasian fly way, so a variety of wintering migrants like Godwits and Sandpipers stop here to feed. It was July when we were there, so the migrants had not yet arrived from the Northern hemisphere.

The star of the sanctuary is the Black swan, a bird exclusive to Australia. Once found in New Zealand also, it was shot out of existence there, and was then re-introduced. It is an arrestingly graceful bird, with a bright red beak and white wing feathers that are revealed dramatically in flight.

As far as eye could see, there were black swans in a dreamlike tableau. The silence that pervaded the area added a touch of surreal to the scene. If you strained your ears you could hear the hissing sound of the swans. Binoculars revealed some swans with cygnets. Evidently, they were breeding here. These birds mate for life and both male and female share parental chores. A particular variety of algae that grows in this lake is what attracts the swans. In one year, birdwatchers counted 12,000 swans in this lake. The only other such breathtaking sight of congregation of birds I have seen is that of flamingos in Lake Nukuru, Kenya.

The first time I set my eyes on a Black swan at close quarters was in the seventies in Ward Lake, Shillong. A pair was in the lake in the centre of the town as virtual captives with wing feathers clipped. Undeterred, they built a nest among the reeds in preparation for breeding. A keen birder, Nari Rustomji, Chief secretary of Meghalaya, kept a daily eye on the swans on his way home from office, making sure that the birds got police protection round the clock. In time, four cygnets arrived and the family of six proved a major attraction in that hill station.

The Jervis National Park sanctuary is close to the beach resort town of Culbarra, so the stress on the area is high. Among all ecosystems, it is the wetland that is highly vulnerable to pressures. In the 1950s, there was a move to reclaim this lagoon to build houses as part of the beach town. Frances Bray, an ardent birder who lived in Culbarra, opposed the move, organized a campaign and eventually redeemed the lake for the birds and for posterity. Even today, the pressure can be seen and she is still actively defending the lake. A developer has submitted a proposal for a golf course by the side of the lake. Realizing that the runoff of organic material and fertilizers would spell doom of the lake, Ms. Bray is busy arranging meetings. There is also a proposal to declare the lake a Ramsar site.

I checked the birds I had logged in Wollumboola that day; there were two lifers in the list, birds I had seen for the first time in my life. One was a Gannet which I saw in flight; the other a Masked plover, a bird reminiscent of our Yellow-wattled lapwing, but slightly larger. Before we left the place, from a viewing point we watched a lone Harbor seal frolicking in the water. He had the ocean to himself.

–

The Hindu
(01.10.2011)

The Dipper

Skirting the small hill on which our house in Shillong stands, flows a stream. Alongside is a road which spans the stream by a wooden bridge at one point. After a spot of jogging one morning, I was leaning on the railing catching my breath and contemplating the stream when a Brown dipper, a chocolate coloured bird of myna size with a stump tail, flew in and sat on a rock, my first sighting of a dipper about whose strange ways I had only read in bird books. Then every morning I looked out for the dipper and found it at different points in the stream, always active. At one point, the stream comes out of a large tube under a culvert, creating a small waterfall. I often spotted the dipper here. At times, it would go behind the sheet of water and emerge after a few minutes.

The dipper is an extraordinary bird. Actually an insect-eating, songbird like the Magpie robin, it has found an ecological niche in the aquatic world, feeding on water insects, tadpoles and similar small life that inhabit streams. To enable it to survive in this chosen area, for which it is not really equipped, some ingenious modifications have taken place in its body… like the car in the film *Chitty Chitty Bang Bang* which, if you remember, takes off into the air with some extra fittings. But the changes in the dipper are not quite complete. An ornithologist calls this bird "one of Nature's recent experiments."

Its plumage is soft with a rather heavy layer of down feathers. The preen gland, which provides oil to keep the plumage waterproof, is ten times larger than of other insect-eating birds. A flap over the nostrils keeps water out when the bird dives. A very thin membrane over the eyes, working like a draw curtain, protects them. Its feet, however, are not webbed but still the bird swims, though rather clumsily, on the surface.

But underwater, it is an expert swimmer and can go as deep as six metres. In these "submarine" flights it uses its wings. What is most fascinating in the feeding method of the dipper is not the fact that it dives deep, but actually walks along the bottom of the stream looking for larvae and insects sticking to rocks. It remains submerged merely by tilting its body at an angle as the force of the current keeps it down.

This probably is the reason why it prefers to live by fast running mountain streams rather than stagnant pools. You see them only in streams up to even 5000 metres high in the Himalayas. Severe cold does not bother them. On several winter mornings as the carpet of frost crackled under my feet, I watched the dipper plummet into water with great abandon, come out a few seconds later, shake off the water and dive in again.

The dipper is distributed all over the world and in India we have two varieties: The Brown dipper (what I saw) and the White-breasted dipper of the Himalayas. They are loners and the only time you can see a dipper in the company of another will be during breeding season, when they build dome-like nests of moss and grass in the crevices of rocks, very close to water. This is the time they come out with their trilling song.

Having seen the dipper so many mornings, I thought I should share the delight with others and through *The Newsletter for Birdwatchers* invited bird buffs sojourning in Shillong to come and take a look. Some responded. Whenever we made our way to the stream, the dipper was present, hopping from rock to rock, bobbing, diving and frolicking, healing our life's many little wounds.

–

The Hindu
(17.06.1979)

White-rumped Shama

Common cranes

Pheasant-tailed Jacana

Crowned crane

Ground hornbill

Blue-tailed Bee-eater

Andaman Coucal

Pied crested cuckoo

Painted storks

Spot billed pelicans

Frog Mouth

Harris Falcon

Black swans

Brown Dipper

Mammals And Reptiles

The Blackbuck Of Vistarpura

The Rabaris, who are nomadic pastoralists, had camped in the middle of an expanse near that village in central Gujarat. Three dogs from their camp set off and gave chase to a herd of blackbuck that I had been watching. In a breathtaking display of litheness and agility, the buck took off, sailing into the air effortlessly and keeping a safe distance between the dogs and themselves. The dogs soon lost wind and stopped. The buck stopped too and started grazing again until the dogs were ready for pursuit. This recurred a couple of times, but the dogs could never get anywhere near and the buck did not leave that field. I recalled what M. Krishnan had written many years back. "If you like speed and want to see something sustained in its effortlessness, rhythmic impetuosity, you should watch a herd of blackbuck going all out for a few miles; there is tangible, real speed for you."

Though I could not observe them go like that for miles, I got an idea of their power and speed in those fields near Vistarpura village, about 60 kilometres from Ahmedabad. The story of their presence here, where there is no forest and among the villages, is a heartening piece of conservation by people. In 1971, a herd of blackbuck, about twenty-five, presumably from Rajasthan, appeared around the village Vistarpura. Though they strayed into cultivated fields, the farmers did not disapprove, but informed the Forest Department, who moved in swiftly. With the cooperation of the villagers who belong to the Swami Narayan sect, popular in this part of the country, the foresters protected the buck.

The only threat the buck faces here is the occasional gun-wielding poachers who come from towns. But they rarely escape the watchful eyes of the farmers. A count done in 1996 showed that there are more than 2000 buck here, spread over fifteen villages. In a few places, the village common has been earmarked as pastureland for these animals where the Forest Department raises grass. A few months ago the Minister of Environment and Forests of Gujarat visited the village and honoured the fifteen headmen of the villages that have been caring for the herds of blackbuck. A lump sum grant is given as compensation to the village panchayats for any damage the buck may cause to standing crops.

Blackbuck, India's only true antelope, is also exclusive to this country. The does and the fawns are yellowish, while the adult buck is black above and sports those magnificent spiral horns. It could easily outrun its only predator, the cheetah, which, unlike the blackbuck, could not sustain its speed over long distances. The blackbuck is essentially an animal of the plains, scrub jungle and grasslands. Its Tamil name is *Veli man* (Buck of the open) is thus apt. They are ideally equipped for such a habitat. An attempt to introduce them into Mudumalai sanctuary in the Nilgiris in 1958 ended in failure.

It was in grassland, somewhere in Africa, that humans evolved and it is the grassland that still provides much of our food. Many of our cereal crops are just modified grass. Once humans started cultivating grasslands, a habitat began to disappear and the creatures exclusive to this locality began to vanish too. But the sad thing is that much of the grassland that went under plough in recent years is not being used to increase food production but to raise cash crops like tobacco, peanuts and sugar.

Grasslands develop where the soil is too thin and the rainfall too meagre for trees to grow, but sufficient to prevent the emergence of desert. And where there are large herds of cattle, as it has been the tradition in Gujarat, the animals feed on the seedlings and ensure that trees do not come up. As you travel across this part of the country you still see patches of grassland and get an idea of what it would have been before they were taken over for agriculture. There are still some areas of grassland in Kutch and Bhavnagar. But the best known among the grasslands is Velavadar, which is now a sanctuary for about 2500 blackbuck. This area was once the private grazing ground, called *vidi*, of the Maharajah of Bhavnagar.

Even during the turn of the century, blackbuck could be seen in large herds as one travelled in the train from Mumbai to Ahmedabad. Now they survive only in a few sanctuaries like Point Calimere in Tamil Nadu, Ranebennur in Karnataka and Velavadar in Gujarat. Loss of habitat and hunting have spelt its doom. It has been the most hunted animal in India, both for meat and for trophies. The spiral horns of the male buck were used as weapons. Traditionally they were hunted with trained cheetahs until shot-gun wielding "sportsmen" appeared on the scene. Large scale decimation went on during the British period. *The Dharwad gazetteer* records an instance in which a British officer bagged 34 buck in a day's shoot.

That morning, I saw at least five different herds in different villages, including an albino female blackbuck, grazing contently. In the proximity of well-meaning villagers, these herds have grown comparatively tame. If you are a wildlife photographer, there is a slight change in the rules here. You have a better chance of getting closer if you are in white dress, for that is what the Gujarati farmers wear: white *Khediyon* above and *Chorno* below, complete with a white turban.

–

The Hindu
(02.05.1996)

The Defiant One

It had rained the previous night, an unusual winter rain. With mist still hanging over the tree canopy, the jungle looked magical. We were on the mud track that snaked through the Sal forest in the Kanha Tiger Reserve. When we negotiated a bend, we saw an adult gaur drinking off one of the puddles on the road. We stopped. The gaur took its time to drink, then turned and stood in the middle of the road, looking at us. The driver drove close, hoping that it would move away. No. It did not move but simply stood. In Kanha, the rules of the sanctuary are followed strictly. No honking. The driver reversed and we waited. A Rocket-tailed drongo kept up a concert in varied notes, like a medley. From a distance a Red-jungle fowl called.

It is amazing what you can achieve if all the visitors and sanctuary staff follow the rules in letter and spirit. One rule is that no one gets off the vehicle inside the sanctuary. So over the years the resident animals and birds have grown trusting. They seem to accept vehicles as a harmless something. The moment the profile of the vehicle changes, like a hand protruding, there is problem. They seem to distrust human beings, the bipeds. Claude Martin, who had studied the Swamp deer of Kanha in the 1970s was with us in the jeep. He told me that he used to swim across Banjar river that flows through the sanctuary. There were occasions when he stood immobile with just his head above water; the deer, and sometimes even a tiger, did not bother when they came to drink. Another rule is that the jeep should never go off the mud track. The drivers here follow this scrupulously.

Located in the Satpura ranges, the Kanha Tiger Reserve has been protected since 1933. Now, all its wealth is showcased in this vast stretch of moist deciduous forest, interspersed with grass lands which sustain the Barasingha, a large deer endemic to this forest. But it is for its tiger population that Kanha is known and attracts visitors from the world over. This was one of the first nine reserves to come under Project Tiger when it was implemented in 1973. Later, the sanctuary was expanded, basically by repatriating the villages in the periphery. In a unique move, the money collected from tourists is ploughed back to the development of these resettled villages. In the forest we see evidences of a village like a platform around a banyan tree or the remains of a brick house, overgrown with creepers. Many youngsters from the local Gond tribe work as guides. Their bush craft and knowledge of natural history is remarkable. Even without binoculars, our guide could identify each bird just by its flight pattern or silhouette.

This stretch of forest teems with ungulates, including the gaur. Often mistakenly called the bison, the gaur is a wild ox – unlike the bison which is a buffalo. Flourishing all over India in dense forests, its only enemy in the jungle is the tiger, which can bring down even a full-grown gaur. Once hunted for its horn and meat, gaur is one of the very visible ungulates of this sanctuary. After that day we were to see a large herd of gaur, about thirty heads, close to the sanctuary entrance .

The gaur blocking our path continued to stand still, like a gigantic ebony carving. To see this magnificent animal so close is always a stirring experience. Meanwhile one more jeep full of tourists joined us. After what appeared to be a long time, our driver hit upon an idea. He opened the jeep door a few inches and slammed it shut. The noise, quite out of place in the forest, startled the stoic gaur. He moved rather reluctantly and started walking downhill.

–

The Hindu
(09.03.2008)

The Macaques Of Puduthottam

Sometime in the 1930s, a British officer visiting Courtallam falls in Tamil Nadu spotted a troop of Lion-tailed Macaques foraging on the rock face of the Main falls, even as many pilgrims bathed below. This incident is cited to make the point that these highly endangered primates were not always as shy of humans as they are now. Sadly, there is no trace of them anywhere in the Courtallam ranges now. There are some troops in Kalakad sanctuary, about 60 kilometres from Courtallam.

It seems these primates have come full circle, thanks to the strict protection they have enjoyed in the last five decades. Recently while at Iyerpadi estate near Valparai, right inside Annamalai Tiger Reserve, we came across a troop of LTM going about their foraging chore in the vicinity of Puduthottam estate, often coming close to human beings in the main road. Nature Conservation Society, a Mysore-based outfit which has a unit in Valparai with the goodwill of some planters, has placed two men to take care of these troops, mainly to prevent road kills. These two men are now a part of the landscape and are fondly referred to by the locals as the "Minders of monkeys"(*Kurangu pathukiravanga*). Traffic has been steadily increasing on this road that cuts through Puduthottam estate and there have been casualties of macaques.

LTMs are endemic to the Western Ghats and their habitat is restricted to some patches of dense evergreen forests that thrive in folds and valleys of mountains, in Tamil Nadu, Kerala and Karnataka. After India gained Independence, a large number of hydroelectric projects were built, pilgrimage centres grew in popularity and roads were laid, dissecting the forests that had remained inviolate for millennia.

As their habitat began shrinking fast, the number of macaques living in the wild plummeted. In addition, they were killed for meat, for pelage, for use in native medicine and for pet trade. This picturesque macaque, much-fancied as a cage animal, was kept as a pet in houses of landlords around this area.

This iconic primate has specially evolved for life in the South Indian evergreen rain forests. Of the twelve species of macaques, only the LTM is exclusive to tropical rain forests and are truly arboreal. Omnivorous, they eat insects and birds' eggs in addition to fruits and berries. As much of its home ranges – the rain forests of Western Ghats – have been destroyed, the LTM is one of the world's rarest of mammals, with only around 3000 left.

We spent an hour observing these fascinating primates, frolicking as a troop, picking coffee berries or trying to examine our car. The last time I set my eyes on them was in Kozhikamuthi shola near Topslip, way up on the canopy of a tall tree. Here in Iyerpadi they seemed to be quite used to the proximity of humans, like their forebearers in Courtallam. We could often hear their endearing baby-like calls as they kept in contact with other troop members. They are given to moving through the canopy, hardly coming down to terra firma. But when a road splits the shola, they have to come down to get to the other side and sometimes get hit by speeding vehicles. The Forest department and The Nature Conservation Society have connected the tree canopies from either side of the road through bamboo bridges to enable macaques to cross over without coming down to the road.

A kaani tribal in Kalakad-Mundanthurai sanctuary tells us that the Tamil name of LTM is *Solai mandhi* (monkey of the rainforest), as different from *Karu mandhi* (Black monkey, Nilgiri langur). Long before the Englishman arrived on the subcontinent, all these animals were known to our people and had been given appropriate and meaningful local names. Most of these names have disappeared from parlance and now we resort to translating these incongruous English names into local languages.

These patches of shola forests (*solai*) in Tamil Nadu have very evocative names. Here are some examples: *Yanaikundhi solai* (Where the elephant squatted) *mathikettan solai* (Of the fellow who got fooled) *Kozhikamuthi Solai* (Where the jungle fowl was trapped) and *Karian solai* (The black fellow) A toponymic study of these names can reveal fascinating insights about human-forest interaction.

Human beings have effectively modified the environment to suit their requirements. But animals, by and large, have to adapt to prevailing environmental conditions. Dr. Yukimaru Sugiyama, a Japanese primatologist who came to study this monkey in 1961, warned that the Lion-tailed macaques were on the verge of extinction. Ten years later, Steven Green from New York spent more than a year at Kalakad area; when he sounded his word of caution, it was received with skepticism. However, his report led to the protection of that area and the Government announced scrapping of a hydroelectric project near Kalakad to save the habitat of these primates.

Close on the heels of Green's report came the campaign to save the Silent Valley in Kerala, one of the habitats of the macaques. This 1973 campaign was one of the earliest of its kind in the country, and big guns like Salim Ali joined it. It gave rise to the interesting "Man-Monkey" debate, which somewhat trivialized the issues involved. Eventually the scheme was given up and the area declared a national park. Now it is part of the Nilgiri Biosphere.

In the nineteen eighties, Ajith Kumar studied the LTMs in Topslip near Pollachi and extended our understanding of these macaques. This Bengaluru-based primatologist cautioned that we should not get a misleading picture by the easy sighting these rare monkeys. The number of all varieties of monkeys is going down, he says, as rampant destruction of forests continues the world over. The LTMs now live in small patches of fragmented rain forests, marooned, amidst sprawling tea estates that are exposed to barrels of lethal pesticides. It is as if they live in ever shrinking tiny islands and this insularity makes their prospect of survival dim in spite of tough regulations.

–

The Hindu
(01.06.2012)

Go Unto The Ant…

Carl Sagan once said that most of us go through life as if there is no external world. We do not stop to observe the myriad creatures that share this earth with us. And one living thing that goes almost unnoticed, in spite its omnipresence, is the humble ant.

With the growth of sociobiology as a discipline, this insect has received considerable scientific attention. The study of ants has developed as a branch within the larger field of entomology and acquired its own name: Myrmecology. New technological tools provided further momentum for this study. Now, two young myrmecologists have come up with a dazzling new book that opens up a whole new world. The authors' concern about ants is part of their commitment to make Natural History popular among non-specialists.

The story of this book itself is a saga of perseverance. The authors, both scientists, decided to campaign for an increased awareness about ants. They lament that these ubiquitous creatures do not get much mention in popular science literature. They point out that other than the ground-breaking work by Lt. Col. Bingham, *Ants and Cuckoo-Wasps of British India*, published as part of the Fauna of British India series in 1903, there has been no study on this subject. The twosome decided to fill this gap and began work on a book on ants. This was to serve the double purpose of celebrating their decade of ant-watching and also to commemorate the centenary of Bingham's book. They raised money through donations from wildlife enthusiasts, collected photos from wildlifers, and networked with ant-specialists all over the world. The book took shape as a collective effort.

The book is divided into two parts. The first gives an overview of the world of ants and details of life in the colony. It incorporates the latest findings on the subject. The second is a field guide that describes the species and provides keys to identify them. The fascinating world of ants is captured in colour and ink drawings. The authoritative text portrays in detail the life and activities of ants that form an important dimension of Earth's biodiversity: There are 11,931 known species of ants, varying in size from 40 mm to 1 mm. About 25% of the total animal biomass of this world is made up of ants. The remarkable aspect of ants is that they are social insects; they divide their work in the colony and this division of labour is based on factors such as age, social interaction and even size. What we read about the organization and work in a colony of ants is bound to change our anthropometric way of seeing this world.

Ants are everywhere, having colonized varied habitats in all corners of Earth, including our homes. Particularly plentiful, endemic in tropical countries, they are absent only in extremely cold areas like the Antarctica. They occupy wide-ranging ecological niches, like the canopies of trees in rain forests, subterranean burrows and rotting logs. Thus do they make maximum use of available resources. They are now being recognized as ecological indicators, like birds. For instance, the presence of closed canopy specialists (species that nest in leaf litter) indicates the pristine and undisturbed nature of that forest. Over millennia, ants have evolved symbiotic relationships with plants. They pollinate and even disperse seeds. Some sap-sucking aphids are protected by ants like a security agency.

The authors point out that ants have evolved along with other creatures, plants and animals. There is a tree that develops a hollow cavity in its trunk to enable a species of ants to establish its colony. In the tropical forests of Southern India, a certain species of arboreal ant builds a large abode, called Pagoda nest. They create this carton-like nest on trees, by chewing leaves and mixing them with secretions from their salivary glands. In this carton, the Rufous backed woodpecker lays its eggs. The ants, though of the predator variety, do not attack the eggs or nestlings.

Ants navigate through a complex chemical trail left by the other ants. When they move in a single file, you will notice it is never in a straight line. When an ant stands guard at the entrance to its colony, it relies on chemical traces to confirm that each ant entering belongs to the same clan.

Chemicals play a crucial role in the lives of ants, and humans have benefited by studying this. Ants use certain chemical to preserve their food, and prevent it from being spoilt by fungi. This element is now used in the pharmaceutical industry. Just like the dance of the bee, the behaviour of ants also provides scientific insights.

The illustrations support the text admirably. The line drawings and cartoons have been done with the minimalism that brings Japanese paintings to mind and sharply focus on the subject at hand. They serve the purpose for which they have been drawn extremely well. The keys and signages are imaginative and appropriate, which makes the field guide part very user-friendly indeed. Nearly 50 species of ants found commonly in Peninsular India are introduced. The section on each species is illustrated with a photograph, making identification easy.

Digital technology has extended the frontiers of nature photography, particularly micro work. It has been fully utilized in this work which carries about 150 photographs. The pictures by Ajay Narendra and S. Karthikeyan (known for his butterfly photographs) are remarkable. Insect photography is tricky. There are issues with light for one thing. One is working with high magnification, any mistake will also be overblown. So one has to ensure extra stability. The subject is on the move all the time and you have to juggle with very little depth of field. I was particularly impressed by Kalyan Varma's photograph of an ant stinging an aged queen bee to overthrow her. We are told that the coup was successful.

The authors' concern about ants is part of their commitment to make natural history popular among non-specialists. There is even a thoughtful note on making artificial nests for ants so that you can observe their life. It is evident that close attention has been paid to designing the book, an aspect that is often neglected in India. The colours chosen, the fonts used, the paper selected and the layout—all point to the care given by the publishers. It is a delight to handle this book, which is an inspiring example.

This is indeed a milestone publication, much as Salim Ali's *The Book of Indian Birds* published in 1937. In the otherwise carefully crafted work, an obsolete name like Pariah kite sticks out. Not only is there a new name for this bird, the derogatory prefix has even been yanked off the Oxford Dictionary.

The book leaves untouched the whole corpus of lore, mythology and fables related to ants in our country. The sthalapurana of the late Chola temple in Tiruverumbur near Tiruchirappalli has an interesting story connected with ants. The devas, frightened of the belligerent asuras, took the form of ants and daily climbed the small rocky hill on top of which stands the temple to worship. Moved by this devotion, Siva, the deity in this temple, assumed the name Erumbeswarar or Lord of Ants. Whence came the name. Tiruverumbur (The village of Ants) to the village. A poem from the medieval Tamil anthology Ahananooru talks of poor people breaking up an anthill to get the grains stored by ants. And proverbs. The one that comes to my mind first is a Tamil one – Erumboora kal kuzhiyum – By the constant trail of ants, even a rock can get worn.

–

On a Trail with Ants. A Handbook of Ants of Peninsular India by Ajay Narendra and M. Sunil Kumar, Bengaluru 2006, Paperback with 150 colour plates. Pages 193. Price Rs. 600.

Frontline

(01.02.2008)

To Kill An Elephant

One of the purposes of an anthology such as the one under review, is to resurrect our print heritage. In a tropical country like ours, the climate is not kind to books. So an anthology provides the present-day reader access to pieces from rare tomes stored in vaults of archives. Otherwise, where else can one read F. W. Champion, a forester who was writing about the thrills of wildlife photography even as his compatriots were blazing away in Indian jungles? Or Douglas Hamilton, the man who explored the Annamalai ranges of the Western Ghats and left valuable documents on the paradise we lost?

However, of the thirty-nine pieces in this collection, twenty-nine are on hunting elephants, on how the white hunter went about shooting these hapless creatures. Some pieces read like how-to-do manuals. Of all the blood sports, I think the most cruel is elephant hunting. It is a harmless animal, an easy target, has a close-knit relationship with other members of its herd, and is specially dear to Indians. There is no tradition of elephant hunting in India. For the white hunter, elephants were just a "big game", shot sometimes for trophy and at other times, just for the heartless pleasure of killing. This book mentions an instance of a party of hunters killing six elephants from one herd in one go.

This kind of "Shikar" (hunting) literature emerged by end of the nineteenth century and is something unique to the Raj. To break the monotony of life in a colony, the British took to hunting, and often recounted stories of their adventures in journals like Blackwood's Magazine. These stories invariably showed the hunter in heroic light. Writers such as Samuel Baker set the trend in 1860 and the writings of Jim Corbett and Hugh Allen remain the apogee of shikar literature. What is important to us is the writers' knowledge of the jungle and its creatures, not the story of killing the quarry. We also have to bear in mind that shikar literature glamourizes hunting and does not serve the cause of conservation. The myth that hunters contributed to conservation has been effectively blown; hunting accounted for 25% of extinctions. Now that shooting is illegal and hunting a dirty word, there will be no more shikar literature. This is the reason why old pieces on shikar keep getting republished. Such writings remain popular because they are in the realm of thrillers, like the James Bond series.

The ten articles that deal with the natural history of elephants are valuable documents indeed. We learn that elephants can swim non-stop for six hours and that the British deployed 150 trained elephants in their attack against Srirangapatna. We get a peep into the state of forests and wildlife of the Indian sub-continent in the 19th and early part of 20th century. The incidental references to other forest creatures gives an idea of the abundance of wildlife in that period. Champion's piece on photographing elephants is a classic, as is his portrait of an annoyed tusker. The editor has thoughtfully retained the original spellings, which adds to the period flavour. The line drawings, cartoons and photographs add to this dimension. The book contains two very useful sections for researchers: the glossary of terms used in elephant handling and the bibliography. But the omission of R. Sukumar's work on elephants in the latter is rather glaring.

Some of the articles that find a place here have already been republished in similar Stephen Alter's Great Indian Hunting Stories

(Penguin 1988). Collections such as Champion's book itself have been republished. It is not clear why the editor has restricted the collection to British period. Had he not, readers would have got the benefit of reading M. Krishnan's pieces on elephants of South India, Thomas Trautman's work on elephants in ancient India, P. D. Stracy's writings on the elephants of North Eastern India and more recently, R. Sukumar's much acclaimed observations on the Thalamalai elephants.

–

The Great Indian Elephant Book. Anthology of Writings on Elephant in the Raj. edited by Dhriti K. Lahiri-Choudhury. 1999. Oxford University Press, New Delhi 110001. Pages 459. Rs. 595.

Frontline
(15.02.2001)

Wanderers Of The High Seas

Walking along the water's edge at Tiruvanmiyur beach on a January morning, we saw an Olive Ridley turtle in the throes of death, washed ashore. A closer look revealed that its back flippers had been mutilated, probably by the rudder of a trawler, and it was bleeding profusely. Trawlers are just one of the causes that has pushed this creature to the brink of extinction.

Local fishermen know the Ridleys as "Panguni aamai" as they come ashore to lay eggs in the Tamil month of Panguni (January-February). Year after year, they arrive at the same nesting area, where they often meet their end. The female digs a pit in the sand with her back flippers and drops about 50 to 100 eggs. After 40 to 50 days, the eggs hatch out and the hatchlings instinctively turn towards the sea and find their way to the depths of the ocean. They nest in the same site in large numbers. The largest nesting population of these turtles arrives in Odisha; at Gahirmatha, over 2,00,000 have been counted in one season.

Of the five sea turtles that visit the Indian coasts for nesting, it is the Ridley that has been most exploited. Traditionally they have been hunted and their eggs robbed for the table. During the Raj days, the British in India ate these turtles and their eggs as delicacies. (For more on what the British in India ate, see *The Raj at Table* by David Burton, 1993.) As recently as the late sixties, vendors hawked turtle eggs in the streets of Chennai. Even now, along the East Coast road you come across coastal folks selling turtle eggs.

The surge of enthusiasm for wildlife conservation that swept our country in the early seventies brought the plight of turtles into focus. In 1970, Romulus Whitaker, then managing the Madras Snake Park, was living by the sea and observed the decimation that these reptiles were subjected to. Along with Satish Bhaskar and Jean Delouche, he initiated steps to save the turtles. With volunteers like Anne Joseph and Preston Ahimaz, both from the WWF, he organized what came to be known as "turtle walks". During nesting season, the volunteers walked along the beach at night and collected the eggs, covering the area from Marina to Kalpakkam. According to their estimates, about 14,000 turtles came to the Chennai beaches for nesting. Whitaker and his team persuaded National and Grindlays bank to provide a space in Injambakam, where a makeshift hatchery was set up and the eggs buried under sand to hatch. In 1982, the WWF Tamil Nadu took up and continued the hatchery programme. Soon the Forest Department stepped in and set up three more hatcheries. Whitaker demonstrated what could be done with very little resources and a strong belief in a cause; later he was to prove the same point in the case of crocodiles. The turtle walks are still carried on by the Students' Sea Turtle Conservation Network. In addition to helping the turtles, they continue to win new converts to the cause of conservation.

However, there is a hitch. Biologist Jack Frazier pointed out that the temperature around the eggs during incubation is critical in sex determination. The implication of this finding is immense. It is possible that with all good intentions, we might be releasing hundreds of hatchlings of the same sex into the sea. Whitaker said that newer equipment could control the temperature so precisely that one could determine the sexes accurately. If in a lot of 100 eggs, one want 30 females and 70 males, it could be done.

The Protection of Wildlife Act of 1972 listed the Ridleys as endangered. But it is one thing to provide legal protection and totally another enforcing it. The nesting turtles have to contend against many threats. In the Odisha coast, the nesters and their mates often get tangled in trawler nets and die. Some state governments, such as Odisha and Andhra Pradesh, have enforced the use of Turtle Excluder Device (TED) in trawlers. This one-way flap in the net lets the turtles out and saves them from drowning. This step is yet to be taken in Tamil Nadu.

When the turtles come ashore in thousands, they are vulnerable and can be easily caught. The false belief that the blood of Ridley has medicinal properties leads to a lot of poaching along the shores. As the nesting turtles leave clear tracks in the sand, it is easy to locate and get at the eggs. Stray dogs, that have multiplied in thousands, smell out the nests and plunder them. In the sea also, it is difficult to protect the turtles as they roam the high seas. The "freedom of the seas" policy complicates the matter further. Giant high-tech fishing vessels kill large number of turtles. As chemicals are dumped into the sea and oil spills occur, the turtles fight a losing battle.

However, one point is clear. Massive destruction of breeding adults, which is on now, can alter the situation, even if there is a large population. Just as we have eliminated many creatures from the face of Earth, we could also wipe out some creatures of the ocean also. It is already happening in the case of whales.

–

The Hindu
(19.05.2002)

A herd of Blackbuck

A Gaur in Kanha

Lion-tailed Macaque

Common Red Fire ant

Elephant in Bandipur

HABITATS

Courtallam: Land Of The Lost Orchid

As a student in Palayamkottai in1950s, a trip to Courtallam was always a much-awaited break. On arriving at Courtallam bus stand, we would rush to Tiger hall, our usual stop, drop our bags there and head for the hills. Visitors to the falls were few then and the ranges retained much of their pristine nature. A trek along Puckle's path – named after the Collector who laid it in the 1860s – to Thenaruvi and beyond to the Paradise cave (originally *Paradesi Kugai*) was the high point of the visit.

Courtallam, where the river Chithar (Small river), swelling after the Southwest monsoon in the Pothikaimalai ranges, comes down in a series of cascades, ending with the massive falls, has been known for its therapeutic air. The rain-bearing clouds rushing through Aryankavu pass transform themselves into a fine drizzle that is so characteristic of Courtallam. In the Siva temple near the falls, the deity is ceremoniously anointed with *kashayam* (herbal decoction), as an antidote to constant exposure to drizzle.

When this area passed into the hands of the East India Company after the Poligar wars, Courtallam became a favourite of British officers; the first Collector ofTirunelveli, the legendary Lushington, set up residence here. Subsequent Collectors chose to hold their cutcherry here. Courtallam was recognized as a sanatorium and attracted British officers from all over the presidency. Artist William Daniells came here and sketched the falls. In 1811, the government appointed a committee to find the reasons for its reputation of being so therapeutic. The committee, in its report, extolled the virtues of the climate, the drizzle and commented on the efficacy of a bath in the falls as "…the happy means of rapidly restoring many to health and comfort, who previous to their visit to Courtallam, appeared to be hastening to their graves." But after Kodaikanal, Ooty and Yercaud came up, they became more popular as resorts.

Casamajor, company's resident in Courtallam, introduced exotic varieties of cash crops such as nutmegs, cloves and spices brought in from Moluccas. By 1812, the harvest of fruits and other products from Courtallam found their way to European markets. But competition from Java was fierce and the trade did not catch on. Mangosteen fruits were probably introduced at this time and remain a favoured specialty of Courtallam.

If Western Ghats is a biodiversity hotspot, Courtallam is truly representative of that character of the ranges. The hills are home to a bewildering variety of plants, birds and mammals. In 1835, botanist Dr. Robert Wight collected 1200 species of flowering trees in an area of just 51.8 square kilometres. He estimated that at least 2000 species were present. The variety of ferns was particularly very high. (A three-volume biography of Wight has been brought out by Henry Noltie, chronicler of British India Botanists.)

A very rare orchid, after the shoe-shaped flower *Paphiopedilum drury,* christened after Heber Drury, is endemic to these ranges. Known among orchid fanciers as "the Lost Orchid", it is now a rare collector's item. Heber Drury (1819-72), a Colonel in the Madras Light Infantry stationed in Travancore, wrote the *Handbook of the Indian Flora* (3 vol) and *The Useful Plants of India*. (There was another G. D. Drury, Collector of Tiruvelveli, in 1928, the same officer who dug a canal from Kaviri at Erode). The British government was interested in knowing the commercial potential of the plants in their tropical colonies, while naturalists like Drury were interested in the plants as subjects of study. As an adjunct to this study, a school of botanical painting developed in South India. We have a volume of drawings of grasses made by a "native" artist whom Drury employed while in Travancore. His autobiography *Reminiscences of Life & Sport in Southern India* (London: W.H. Allen & Co., 1890) provides a window in the natural history of the period

"Lady's slipper orchid", a terrestrial orchid, is so named after the shoe-shaped flower, that lies buried underground most of the year, surfaces during flowering season, like a tiny coconut sapling. It grows in the grassy slopes of these ranges and blooms in May-June, a yellow coloured flower of 5-7 cm size. The nearest I got to it this fabled orchid was when I set my eyes on a pressed specimen in the herbarium of the Botanical survey of India, Coimbatore. There was an orchid fancier in Bengaluru who had two plants, but would not trust me enough to let me photograph them. What is special about this plant is that it is one of the relict species; that is, it is a species found in the Himalayas and in the Western Ghats, but nowhere in between. Among mammals, the tahr, and among birds, the Grey-headed flycatcher are relict species.

The lost orchid came to symbolize the disappearing floral wealth and the amazing biodiversity of the Western Ghats. To raise money to save such rare botanical species of the world, plant artist Stone chose to paint the Lost Orchid and sold it to raise money.

Wildlife was once plentiful in these ranges. I read an account of 1932 of a hunting party of Indians in Courtallam, that came across quite a few panthers and did not bother to shoot any. They were saving their ammunition for tigers which were also plentiful. Sambar, the big cat's staple prey, was also in abundance. M. Krishnan has recorded seeing a troupe of Lion-tailed Macaques foraging on the rock face of the Main falls, while many people bathed below. He narrates this incident to prove the point that these black monkeys were not always so shy of humans as they are now. Sadly, no trace of them anywhere in these ranges. There are some troupes of this highly endangered primate in Kalakad sanctuary. The higher ranges of Courtallam were once home for the rare mountain goat: Nilgiri tahr. As elsewhere, all this has been wiped out. A small population of tahr at Agasthya hills has been recorded.

Birds still abound. If you are a keen birder, the book you should carry on a visit to Courtallam would be *The Birds of Kerala*, now in a new enlarged edition. Walking along the crystalline brooks up the hill, you are sure to hear the magical call of the Malabar Whistling thrush. If you are lucky, you will get a glimpse of it taking off from the rocks and disappearing into vegetation. You could still spot Ruby-throated bulbul, Fairy Blue bird and Green Imperial pigeon. But the Great Indian Hornbill, once a common sight here, has gone the way of the lost orchid.

When I first learnt about this orchid in the early 1970s, I was naïve enough to think that all one had to do is to walk around in this area to see the plant. I went searching for it. In Courtallam, I took the Puckle's path, which goes along the Chithar right up to the awe-inspiring Thenaruvi (Honey falls). Beyond that, I walked up to Paradesi cave (because it is near Paradise Estate) which contains an inscription yet to be deciphered. That was a memorable trek. But I did not see the orchid. It was only later that I learnt that this is a plant of grasslands, and this terrestrial orchid is noticeable only during the flowering season. There are quite a few of this variety in the Himalayas and the North-East but only one in Western Ghats.

Last time when I was in Courtallam in 1974, I got on to Puckle's path as quickly as I could, leaving the milling concourse behind. I walked up to Thenaruvi, far more majestic and awesome than all others in these ranges, and managed to reach Paradise cave. I gazed at the mysterious inscription as yet undeciphered, on the wall of the cave, chiseled millennia ago by some Buddhist or Jain monk who sat there contemplating the meaning of life.

–

The Hindu
(07.08.2008)

Death Of An Estuary

The principle cause for the loss of species is the alteration of the ecosystem in which they live.

-David. W. Ehrenfeld in *Conserving Life on Earth.* 1972

What is an estuary? Where the fresh water of a river meets the brackish water of the sea, it creates a habitat that is midway between land and sea, where the ebb and flow of the tidal currents work on the soil in a timeless rhythm and make it a dynamic ecosystem… that is an estuary. A breeding area for many aquatic lives, it is also the feeding ground for hosts of birds specially equipped to operate in mud flats. This habitat is dominated by fine sedimentary material, brought into the estuary by the tidal flow and this forms the mud flats. With the constant change of salt and freshwater, it is never static. Biologists point to the estuary as the most productive habitat that throbs with small lives of many varieties: frogs, mollusks and diatom. At the mouth of the estuary, a horseshoe-shaped sand bar is formed, with the open side facing the river. And this bar acts as a dam, creating a temporary lake during low tide. The characteristic feature of an estuary is its shallowness, just a few inches of water. During low tide, vast stretches of the riverbed are bared and for the visiting birds, it is a gourmet restaurant, a distinct and fragile habitat created by eons of natural process.

Nothing is more symbolic of our utter disregard for natural heritage as the destruction of the Adyar estuary. Most of the swampy areas and lakes of the city, such as the Spur tank and the Vyasarpadi lake, had been overwhelmed by urban sprawl. But those wetlands were reclaimed when we did not have much idea about the awesome interconnections in environment, between reclamation of lakes and water shortage. But the Adyar estuary survived till recently. It is not just a bird refuge; it's an open space for the city, a wetland that takes care of your subterranean water table and a unique geographical feature. It is one important dimension of the physical identity of the city.

It takes millennia to shape an estuary and we have ruined it overnight by deciding to dredge it to facilitate boating. The islets and delta creeks on the western side of the Thiru. Vi. Ka. bridge have already been cleared. Before long, it will be an urban wasteland. If it had been given protection as a sanctuary, it would have attracted a lot more tourists – if that were the purpose – than a few boats would ever do. And we would have had a heritage intact like Panaji where the estuary right in the middle of the city is a bird sanctuary, attracting hordes of tourists.

Known also as Chengalpattu River, the Adyar river's estuary once extended up to Foreshore estate, encompassing Quibble Island. Consisting of grassy islands, swampy stretches and mangrove-covered bank, the estuary was an incubator for aquatic life. It has been polluted for a long time. The massive laundry operations that began nearly a century ago near Marmalong Bridge, the upstream industrial effluents and the sewage of the city defiled the river. Still, the tidal dynamics kept the estuary habitable and birds continued to come, though the numbers were reduced progressively in recent years.

In the wake of the Stockholm Conference of 1972, as the world was swept by an awareness of its natural heritage and the speed with which it was disappearing, certain bird enthusiasts in South

Madras – R. Sukumar (who has made his reputation as Asia's elephant specialist), Selvakumar (who studied gaur in Mudumalai) and writer Siddhartha Buch – began looking at the Adyar estuary standing on the wrought-iron walkway of the old Elphinstone bridge. They realized that the estuary offered a fascinating insight into the natural world for the city-dwellers and should be preserved. S. Jagadish, a student of a city college (now a doctor with the RAF), studied of the estuary for a Science project in 1975. News of the astonishing bird wealth of the area spread. The Madras Naturalist Society formed in 1978 was greatly concerned about the estuary and took Salim Ali to see the spot for himself.

Efforts were on to declare it a sanctuary. The WWF India and later INTACH backed this appeal. One of the objections was its proximity to the airport. This argument does not carry any weight for two reasons. One is that most of the birds that pose a threat to airplanes are highflying kites that live on offal, not the small waders that visit a marsh. Second, there are bird refuges close to airports in many parts of the world; immediately adjacent to the Kennedy airport in New York, separated only by a wire fence, is the Jamaica Bay Wildfowl refuge. However, a signboard came up near the Adyar estuary banning trapping and shooting birds. That is as far as we got. But that did not change the legal status of the estuary in any way.

In the migratory season, waterfowl of different varieties, thousands of sandpipers and shanks and varieties of ducks flock to this feeding ground. Chennai-based ornithologist V. Shantharam, watching the birds of Adyar estuary for many years, says that at least seventy-three species of migratory birds visit this spot. The Little stint, a tiny winter visitor, comes all the way from Eastern Europe and remains till the end of the March. The flocks of tiny birds that fly across like a thin cloth being swept by wind, over the bridge when you are returning home from work, are Sandpipers which are migrants from paleartic region. The most visible bird is the Black-winged Stilt that comes in thousands. These are long-legged birds that stand silhouetted, like cardboard cutouts, in the evening light. During winter, twelve species of terns have been sighted here. I have observed flamingos here; they come from their breeding ground in the Rann of Kutch. Many resident birds can also be spotted here like the Yellow-wattled lapwing and the Common Bee-eater. Rare plants like mangroves bordered the estuary. In fact, some remnant of these mangroves still persists on the Theosophical Society side. All this would be soon gone, making way for boats, if you please.

Whenever we think of tourism, two things seem to spring to our mind: toy trains and boats. The tragic instance is the toy train around Kodaikanal lake (dismantled later following a court decision, thanks to the alertness of a local NGO). And the boats have appalling safety standards. I have not seen a boat in which life jackets are provided to the tourists. Anyone who has visited our monuments and other tourist spots would tell you that what we need is conveniences such as clean toilets and polite employees.

The Adyar estuary is a textbook case of a fragile natural heritage losing out while pitted against frenzied urbanization, a process that has gone through in many cities. Of all the habitats, wetlands are particularly susceptible to such threats from the land hungry. Still, there are instances in India where people have resisted such exploitation and averted long term loss to the city. In Mumbai, the Mahim creek was similarly threatened, but a very articulate environment movement there prevented it. Right in the heart of Pune, the Mulla-Muktha bird sanctuary was established. In Delhi, NGOs went to court and redeemed the greenery of the Ridge. In Chennai the story was different. This raises a larger question… Why is there no environmental movement in Tamil Nadu?

–

The Hindu

(12.01.2003)

New Year At Gopalsamibetta

In the Northeastern periphery of Bandipur National Park stretches a range of hills called Gopalsamibetta (1468 m) that takes its name from the temple on top. It was to this place we headed on the thirty-first of December in 2000, keeping up with the family tradition of ushering in the New Year in a forest. It was late afternoon when we arrived there, having left Mysore after a leisurely breakfast.

This hill temple, dedicated to Lord Vishnu, is under worship, though the devotees who come up here are very few. The brick and mortar shed meant for the temple chariot is now occupied by a posse of police of the Special Task Force. It was formed to catch Veerappan, the bandit, who has been operating in the forests of Bandipur and surrounding areas for more than ten years. They had set up a radio station in the shed. A wall of huge granite boulders had once surrounded the temple. Beyond the temple, remnants of massive battlements can be seen. There is a lookout post with a clear view of the Mysore-Ooty highway snaking across the dry plains.

What is intriguing is that across the next hill runs a wall of immense proportions with an opening in one end. Against whom or what was this wall built? When? Later, thumbing through *Mysore Gazetteer*

(1897) at the Mythic society library in Bengaluru, I learnt that this fort, known as Bettekotta (hill fort), was built by a poligar Somanna Danayaka in the later part of the 18th century. He is one of the nine Danayaka brothers of tradition. (Poligars – anglicized version of the Tamil term *Palayakarar* – were the vassals of the Nayaks of Madurai. Some of them offered resistance to the East India Company but were quickly put down.) Quite a few forts in this area are attributed to these brothers. One such was submerged when the dam across the river Bhavani near Sathyamangalam was built and a huge reservoir came into being.

Close to the temple, on the shoulder of the hill, is a Forest Rest house built in 1933, provided with the barest necessities. No electricity. Like other colonial era rest houses, this one also commands a stunning view of a wide valley on the left and the plains of Gundelpet on the right. A trench – to keep the elephants off – encircles it. Inside the rest house, a large photograph of a hunting party with a slain tiger in the foreground adorns the wall. Closer examination reveals the slayer in the centre of the group as none other than Lord Irwin, Viceroy of British India. The Maharajas of Mysore and Bikaner flank him dutifully. A tiger hunt was something Indian kings organized to honour their imperial guests, a colonial equivalent of a banquet.

After handing over rice and dhal for preparing our supper, we set out on the bridle path that led into the grassland on the other slope. It was mountains and forests all around. The shrill drone of cicadas that pervaded the jungle rose up to a crescendo, stopped abruptly, only to begin tentatively again a few seconds later. The caretaker of the rest house insisted on accompanying us, with his double-barreled breech loader slung rakishly across his shoulders. I did not go into the question of how he was going to protect us with a shotgun from elephants, the evidences of whose presence was all around in the form of heaps of dung.

An outcrop of bare rocks jutting out of the hill, hewn into different shapes by eons of wind and rain, appeared like a sculpture gallery of Henry Moore. From closer, the multicoloured lichen sticking to the rock could be seen. A Brown rock thrush perched on one of the rocks, deftly balancing itself against the wind. On a dead tree stump clung a Rock lizard in an amazing display of camouflage. Even as you were looking at it, it seems to disappear and reappear.

The folds of the valley were clothed in dense forest. You could see the bottom of the fold was like a green ribbon, indicating the presence of a stream. There were many such streams in these parts, and it is here that river Kabini originates. Though most of them were dry now, Ginger lily plants growing at the edge of the forest indicated that the valley had been very wet. Orchids abounded on the trees. We could hear the clear belling of a Sambar from inside the patch of forest in the valley. It is typical Sambar country and home for this deer in vast numbers. Next morning we would spot nearly fifteen of them. This large deer is a favoured prey for tigers.

The ranges of the hills seem to extend endlessly. The slanting rays of the sun accentuated the folds and valleys. The grasslands took on a golden hue as the sun, like a sliver of fire, began sliding behind the ranges. The evening turned cold rapidly. A tenacious lone Black-winged kite was hovering over the grassland even as darkness engulfed the hills. A few stars began appearing tentatively; soon, the clear moonless sky was filled with myriad stars. The Milky Way could be seen distinctly. We hurried back to the Rest House. After an early dinner of rice and a fried dhal of sorts, we snuggled inside our sleeping bags. An occasional belling of Sambar floated from the valley, intensifying the silence of the night.

The crowing of Jungle fowl announced a glorious morning. This magnificent pheasant – nearly shot out of existence a few decades ago for the pot and more for its neck feathers used as fly lure in fly-fishing – is now secure in these sanctuaries. The mist was lifting and morning sun was pouring gold over the landscape. We walked along the ridge of the hill, following a bridle path that cut through the grassland. A Pale harrier, a migrant raptor, had already started scanning the grassland flying low. A Common Sergeant butterfly briefly landed on a clump of grass before setting off to an unknown destination.

We could spot two gaurs in different parts of the hill. Their massive bodies glistened in the morning sun as they grazed contently. When the sun rose a little higher and grew warm, the gaurs disappeared into the forest. It is in the Western Ghats that these bovines attain their maximum proportions. Though these animals are susceptible to diseases like Anthrax and Rinderpest brought in by domestic cattle, and the calves often fall prey to tigers, for now their population is stable. You get to see them easily in all the sanctuaries in the Western Ghats.

There were signs of the presence of other mammals. Brushing up our knowledge of coprology, we could identify droppings of Porcupine and Hare all over. There were three lumps of Tiger scat in different stages of decomposition. The oldest was a just a tight lump of Sambar hair and bones. Scat analysis is a handy tool for wildlife biologists. Learning of the big cat's presence there lent an aura to the place. Bandipur National park was declared a Project Tiger area even when the project was launched in 1973.

Driving back to Bengaluru, we stopped at a wayside dhaba, and as we waited for tea, tallied our bird list. We had sighted seventy-six birds. Though poor compared to the hundred and twenty-five of last New Year at Nagerhole, the consolation for me was that it included two lifers, (birds you sight for the first time in your life): Grey Nightjar and a Black Redstart, a tiny flycatcher that breeds in the Himalayas and winters in the Western Ghats.

–

The Hindu
(15.06.2003)

Kurinji: Flower For The Gods

The Muduvar tribe, who inhabit the mountain ranges around Valparai and Munnar in the Western Ghats, calculate their age with the blossoming of Kurinji flowers. This legendary flower blooms once in twelve years and is due to enliven the mountainscapes.

In the Western Ghats, at an altitude of about 1600 metres, in the region of sholas and grasslands, kurinji flourishes as a gregarious shrub. From the high ranges to Sayadhri Mountains, different varieties of Kurinji flourish in valleys, in slopes and in gorges. All of them have a periodicity from eight to twelve years. After blossoming, the plant wilts and starts growing when the next season comes. Though most of the varieties are blue, there are some yellow varieties also.

Geographers refer to the ranges south of the Palghat gap as Palani ranges and those to the north as Nilgiris. In the Palani ranges, in Mattupatti and Gundumalai around Munnar, Kurinji grows in abundance. In the area around Anaimudi also the plant thrives. Anaimudi, or the Elephant Peak, is the highest point in South India, being several metres higher than the better-known Doddabetta near Ooty. And the area around it is now called Eravikulam sanctuary, home for the Nilgiri tahr. The Indira Gandhi wildlife sanctuary in Tamil Nadu is contiguous to this sanctuary.

Though this flower has been a familiar subject for poets and hill folks, in modern times two British botanists who explored the Palani ranges, Robert Wight in 1836 and Capt. Beddome, in 1857 documented the details and let the wider world know about this plant. The Kurinji found in the Palani and Nilgiri ranges has been christened *Strobulanthus kuntianum*. The Catholic clergy in the Shenbaganur seminary in Kodaikanal kept careful notes of the flowering of Kurinji.

In the Nilgiris, it was only from 1858 that we have records of the years of Kurinji blossoming. A resident of Kotagiri, one Mr. Cockburne had details of the years in which Kurinji blossomed in that area. His father was a pioneer settler in the Nilgiris, whose mother (Cockburne's granny) had talked to the Kotas and Todas and had written down data on Kurinji; thus data from three generations are now available. Around the Nilgiris, this flower is called Nilakurinji and is abundant in Mukurthi sanctuary. In recent years, the Pondicherry-based Salim Ali School of Ecology has been studying the blossoming of Kurinji for several years.

In Tamil Sangam poems (Circa 3-5 AD), there are quite a few references to this flower. In works such as *Agananuru* and *Maduraikanchi*, the plant is referred to as *Karungal Kurinji*, meaning the Black stemmed flower. When it is in bloom, the honey gathered from the hives in that area was valued highly. One poet praises a king as "the one who rules over a country where the Kurinji honey is in plenty."

The Sangam groups of literary works divide the landscape into five categories. The mountainous area was known as Kurinji, after the flower. Murugan, the god of the Kurinji area, wore a garland of Kurinji flowers when he married the tribal girl Valli. This blue flower stands as a symbol for hills and forests. The other landscapes described are *mullai* (jasmine) stands for forests, *marudam* (a tree) stands for pastoral area, *Neythal* (an aquatic flower) denotes coastal area and *Palai* (a tree) represents arid area. In the poetic works, each landscape stands for an emotion or state of mind. Kurinji symbolizes clandestine love or premarital romance. At least one literary work, *Ainkurunooru*, has a hundred poems for each of these landscapes.

The home of Kurinji, which had remained inviolate for millennia, was damaged beyond repair in the last one hundred years. Range after range of forests was cleared for tea, cardamom and timber. To promote leather-tanning industry, Wattle was planted in the heart of Kurinji country. Eucalyptus was grown to supply raw material for rayon and paper. Trees totally alien to this land were brought in and introduced, devastating the ecosystem. Hydroelectric projects submerged vast stretches of virgin rain forests. Now in the little space that is left, in steep valleys and gorges, Kurinji bushes are battling for survival, like many other life forms of the area.

In the last few years, in Kerala and Tamil Nadu, there have been efforts from different quarters to save what is left of Kurinji's home. The Save Kurinji Campaign Council (SAKCIL) founded by Rajkumar, a bank employee, is active in Thiruvananthapuram.

The High Range Wildlife Association, led by a former Planter Chengappa, and The Palani Hills Conservation Council based in Kodaikanal have been campaigning for this plant. Taxonomist Dr. P. K. Mathew of the Society of Jesus, Tiruchi, headed a small committee of the PHCC to draw plans for Kurinji conservation. Mathew's sudden death last April has been a major loss to the conservation movement.

The Kurinji campaigners used to conduct an annual *padayatra* from Kodaikanal to Munnar to gather support for their efforts. The main aim of this campaign is to declare the 95 square kilometres expanse between Kodaikanal and Munnar, at a height of 1600 metres, as a

Kurinji sanctuary. A major portion of the proposed sanctuary lies in Tamil Nadu and the rest in the Idukki district of Kerala. As a part of these efforts, Chennai-based plant artist O. T. Ravindran has been pleading for a stamp featuring Kurinji. He sent a proposal to the Ministry of Communication for a stamp on Kurinji, along with one of his famous paintings of the Kurinji plant, with flowers. Earlier, he had designed a set of four orchid stamps. (In May 2006 a postage stamp featuring a bunch of Kurinji flowers, in Rs.15 denomination was issued by the Department of Post.)

The campaigners point out that here we are dealing with more than just pretty scenery. Kurinji has become a symbol for the biodiverse wealth of Western Ghats, which has been declared one of the eighteen hotspots of the world. The plant also stands for the Lion Tailed Macaque, for Nilgiri tahr, for Nilgiri langur and for the myriads of orchids that share the mountain home. And it is in the Kurinji land that both Vaigai and Amaravathi rivers originate, hence the plea to protect it.

–

The Hindu
(11.09.2005)

Biodiversity In The Backyard

I was on a charpay in a farm by the riverside, when this handsome rooster strode into my view. The long spur on its leg indicated that it belonged to the variety locally called "asali", used in cockfights I have watched as a child. It struck me that I had not seen a farm chicken in years. Its place has been taken over by imported strains, uniform in looks, birds meant for the table. That is the story of most of our indigenous domestic stock. Just as the country's wild biodiversity has been atrophied, our domestic animals and birds have also been disappearing. But the reasons here are different, not loss of habitat.

The Indian subcontinent, known for its abundance of wild biodiversity, is equally rich in the varieties of domestic livestock. Ethologists look upon this area as a major centre of animal domestication. Nowhere is this so striking as in the bovine population. Extensive grasslands, good pasturage and a tradition of professional herdsmen helped the process of evolution of many distinct breeds of cattle. There were grazier communities, like the Rabaris of Gujarat, who moved long distances with their cattle herds. The British were quick to notice the distinct indigenous varieties and divided them broadly into two categories, draught and dairy cattle.

All Indian breeds have certain common characteristics; they are hardy, resistant to diseases, can withstand harsh ecological conditions and subsist on low levels of nutrition. Nearly 26 breeds of cattle have been listed as Indian, which includes well-known breeds such as Gir, Sahiwall, Kankrej, Ongole, Holikar and Kangeyam. Gujarat is the home for some of the prize native breeds. The Kankrej breed with its long horns is identified with the bull featured in the Harappan seal. Even as these stocks stood discounted in India, their merit was realized in South America and a large number of heads were imported, mainly into Brazil, Argentina and Bolivia, where the climate suited them. Now, with advanced technology, frozen semen of certain breeds is exported to these countries from India. I came across a magazine devoted exclusively the Indian breeds of cattle raised in South America. Though the Government has been neglecting cattle of indigenous extraction, some of the princely states took care of specific breeds. The Raja of Jasdan cared for the Gir bulls through his International Gir Breeding Centre and the Kutchi or the Kathiawari horses were bred by the Raja of Gondal.

Unfortunately, we do not have a proper livestock census in our country, so many other highly localized breeds may go undocumented. Only a few years ago, veterinarians identified an indigenous breed of goat in Tirunelveli district in Tamil Nadu. Referred to as Kodivelli breed, this is being revived in the Hosur cattle farm. Similarly, Chegu goats of Himachal Pradesh and Jaffrabadi sheep are very distinct Indian breeds. Nearly 20 distinct breeds of goats have been identified in India, in addition to 42 varieties of sheep. Many of them will be gone in a few years. To care for the native stock, we need authentic data, which is now lacking. We have not thought of any methodologies to save them.

We have at least three varieties of horses in India: Kutchi, Marwari and Manipuri. It is the last variety which was responsible for the development of polo in Manipur. The game then spread to the rest of the world. Kutchi horses are very much in use in Gujarat. The horses you see thundering across the screen in our films – remember the horse-borne bandits in the film *Ali Baba and 40 Thieves* – are all Kutchi. If none else, our film industry will continue to patronize these horses. The identifying mark of this breed is the tips of the ears that almost touch each other. In the museum at Bhuj, Kutch, is a large steel cannon that bears an inscription by Tipu. He had presented this weapon to the king of Bhuj in return for the horses sent to Mangalore by sea. Tipu relied heavily on his cavalry and set up a large stud farm, now known as Hosur cattle farm. We also have our own breeds of camel, like the Malvi breed of Madhya Pradesh. I once witnessed a horse show in Jasdan in which Indian breeds of horses put up an impressive performance. There was even a dancing horse from Marwar. There is an attempt to revive this breed, considered specially suited for show events.

India has one of the oldest canine cultures that have given rise to a variety of distinct breeds of dogs of varied sizes and types. Dog was domesticated in the subcontinent towards to end of Mesolithic period itself. Different geographical areas in India are home to different breeds to suit the respective climates. So we have the Tibetan mastiff in the Himalayas, the Rampur hound in Punjab and the Rajapalayam in Tamil Nadu. Like their European cousins, Indian breeds also have geographical names. During the Colonial period, fascination with foreign breeds worked against the interests of indigenous breeds, which suffered neglect. Kennel clubs did not recognize them. It is only in recent years that certain Indian breeds – Rampur hound, Mudhol – have been recognized and breeding standards laid down. Indian dogs, all oriented to outdoor activity, were used in hunting. Some breeds, such s the Himalayan sheep dog, were trained in herding. Most others were used in guard duty and hunting. We have records of at least one breed being used for military purposes. The Rajapalayam dog was used during the Carnatic wars to attack the British cavalry in their stables. Kombai dogs defended the fort of Marudhu brothers, who ruled from

Kalayarkovil and fought the East India Company forces. One good sign is that more and more Indian dogs are shown in dog shows these days. In the dog shows in Delhi, Tibetan mastiffs, Lhasa Apsos and Rampur hounds are regular participants.

The disappearance of native breeds accelerated after India gained independence. From 1960, cross breeding with exotic cattle breeds was done in order to increase milk productivity. In this process, the indigenous stock got depleted and neglected. And what is more, successive generations of hybrid cattle are yielding less and less milk.

Nowhere is the loss of native strains so apparent as in poultry. The ancestor of all poultry is the Red Jungle Fowl of the North Indian forests. Of the 17 varieties we had, many have disappeared, particularly in the last three decades, such as the Naked neck, once common in our villages. Modern poultry farms went in for exotic hybrids. However, the circle seems to be complete now. The superiority of the country chicken as a table bird and of its eggs is now being realized. Gourmet restaurants have started announcing proudly that they serve country chicken.

–

The Hindu
(16.11.2003)

Kolli Hills: Land Of Honey And Orchids

Dawn had just broken over the hills. In Chemmedu, in Kolli hills near Salem, it is the day for the weekly market. I was at the village common waiting for photo opportunities. From the hamlets around, the hill folk, wrapped in blankets, began arriving one by one with their wares – jack fruits, pineapples, honey, nutmeg, chicken – and started setting up stalls.

Kolli hills, rising abruptly in the middle of the plains of Tamil Nadu, is about 28 kilometres long, lying north south and 18 kilometres wide. On top, the ranges level off into a square shaped plateau. The altitude varies between 1000 and 1500 metres. The ranges receive an average about 1700 mm rain, mostly through the Northeast monsoon, creating ideal conditions for tropical forests to flourish. Not long ago, the ranges were well clothed in forests, but now most of it has disappeared, victim to humanity's paper, building and furniture needs. Still some patches are left in steep valleys and slopes, providing a peep into the past glory of these hills.

While there are so many ranges of mountains in Tamil Nadu, including the mighty Western Ghats, it is the Kolli hills that figure in so many poems in ancient Tamil poetry. In Sangam literature such as *Puranaooru* and *Narrinai*, there are a number of references to these ranges, its people and particularly to their famed king Ori. He was a master archer and one of the seven legendary philanthropist-kings (*vallal*) eulogized in classical Tamil literatures. In *Silapthikaram* there is a mention of a goddess Kolli pavai of these ranges after whom the hills get its name. Poets, particularly Kabilar, talk about the botanical wealth of the hills, the variety of trees and the beauty of the mountainscape, about the elephants and about the herbs. Kambar goes into ecstasies about the quality of honey from these hills.

If there is one striking characteristic of these hills, it is their wealth of biodiversity. Though much of the forest cover has been ravaged, as elsewhere in the country, there is still plenty of nature for one to explore; there are sizable patches of forests left. You could see some as you drive up the picturesque ghat road from Sendamangalam. The forests you see here can be broadly classified into sub-tropical hill forest and dry mixed deciduous forests. The first type appears like rain forest and very little of this type is left, near Ariyur area for instance and it is the second type, which is commonly seen. Trees like rosewood and acacia are still seen, as also some sandalwood trees. Much of the bamboo forests, for which Kolli hills was famous, have been decimated as raw material for paper factories. If you look around carefully, you could see certain varieties of orchids, such as Vanda. Drosera, a rare insect-eating plant, is found in certain areas. The tiny light red flower is the identifying factor for this small plant that spreads along the ground. In recent times, the herbal wealth of these hills has been recognized and the Department of Forests has a few protected areas exclusively for medicinal plants.

Though there are references in classical literature to the tigers and elephants roaming the Kolli hills, none of these large mammals are left now. Occasionally, a sloth bear is sighted. Boars and porcupines seem to be more common. Dhole, locally called *vettaikaran*, is still in the living memory. I was told that there is a small population of the rare Grizzled squirrel, in two valleys. The habitat described is characteristic of mountain streams flanked by tall Marudam trees. But bird life is still abundant. I sighted Emerald green pigeons near the waterfalls.

There are evidences of Jain establishments. Not far from Chemmedu I saw the ruins of a Jain *basti*, complete with a tirthankara statue in the sanctum. In recent days, Arapaleeswarar temple, not far from Chemmedu and going back to Chola days as evidenced by the inscriptions there, has been attracting attention. A picturesque trail leads to the 50-metre-high waterfalls in the same locality which has some dense forests around it.

Unlike the neighbouring Servarayan hills, Kolli hills remained isolated for a long time; it was only in 1961 that a ghat road was laid, replacing the existing mule track. Kolli traders trekked down with their wares to the markets in Sendamangalam and Pelukurichi. A few missionaries, including the legendary Jessie Brand, set up stations in Kolli hills, but not much is known about it outside. (To learn more about this remarkable man and the Kolli hills of last century, read *Climb Every Mountain* by D. C. Wilson).

In the shadow of the mountains nestle a few tiny hamlets, with neatly thatched and square shaped huts, each with a platform around, like a belt. Here live the tribal people of these ranges, Kolli Malayalis, and who belong to the same group as those in Javadhi and Servarayan hills. The legend is that they all come from the same family but were divided into three strands. Mostly farmers and small-time traders, they weave black and white blankets using coarse wool, a distinct trademark of Kolli Malayali people, and doubling as a raincoat in monsoon. In the last hundred years, these hill folks are used to hunting with guns; often these weapons figure in their rituals also.

When I got ready to leave, the sun had risen high lighting up the landscape with its magical brilliance. I could hear the long-drawn call of a Crested serpent eagle setting out on its diurnal hunt. The market was in full swing of activity. Some men moved around with their black and white blankets. One was hawking Kolli honey, now bottled and sealed with a label on it. Kolli hills have managed to retain at least some of their pristine nature. Certainly one reason is that it has not received the kiss of death from tourism.

–

The Hindu
(31.12.2000)

On the Banks Of The Amaravathi

The Amaravathi river swells into life in the Anjanad valley in the Palani ranges of the Western Ghats, whose slopes are awash with kurinji blossoms (*Strobilanthes kuntianum*) once every twelve years. Descending in a northerly direction, it debouches into the plains near Udumalaipettai, Tamil Nadu, and flows by Dharapuram the village where I was born and raised. The name Amaravathi echoes the Buddhist past of this part of the country. In Buddhist mythology, the city of Amaravathi is the capital of Indra's kingdom. A major tributary of Kaveri, this rivers meanders through Coimbatore, Erode and Karur districts.

The man who in modern times explored the area in which Amaravathi originates was a British army officer, Douglas Hamilton. Commissioned to do a survey of the Palani ranges, he stayed in Kodaikanal during 1859-62, camped around the whole range, on valleys and on peaks and drew detailed sketches of the mountainscapes. Later published as sets of lithographs, these sketches are now highly prized collectors' items. Hamilton writes about locating an ancient lake 24 kilometres from Kodaikanal, in the Anjanad valley. Analyzing the geological evidence, he concluded that the eight kilometres long lake was formed as the result of a landslide. From this lake flows the brook that eventually becomes Amaravathi river in the plains. These geological indicators are now lost due to the creation of Berijam, a man-made lake here.

At the area where the Amaravathi leaves the foothills and touches the plains, a dam of masonry and earthen construction was built across it in 1957, impounding water for irrigation and electricity. This is part of a maze of dams and canals in the Palani and Annamalai ranges. These networks of dams, reservoirs, canals and tunnels have spelt disaster to wildlife. They have fragmented the habitats and taken vast stretches of forests underwater. On the far end of the reservoir is a fascinating area known as Thoovanam, literally "drizzle". A landscape of scrub jungle and deciduous forests, it still abounds in wildlife such as elephants and gaur. Further up, the rocky crags are home of Nilgiri tahr, that elusive mountain goat.

Thoovanam area of Amaravathi river is one of the last redoubts of crocodiles in this part of the country, with the large reservoir created by the dam providing them with a good sanctuary. Some of the biggest specimens of muggers can still be seen here. The names of places in this area are picturesque. There is a stream called *Kazhuthai Katti Odai* (the nullah where a donkey was tied). Local tribals say that the name comes from an incident many years ago, when a white planter tied a donkey in this spot as bait to lure a tiger. There is a *Thayirsothu kanavai* (curd rice valley) too.

After passing by what were known during British days as K villages – a series of villages all with names beginning with letter K, such as Karathozhuvu, Kaniyur and Kumaralingam – the Amaravathi is joined by a tributary: the Shanmuganadhi. Here it approaches Dharapuram, my native village.

I decided that on my sixtieth birthday, I should wake up on the banks of this river that formed a backdrop to my childhood years. A tiny farmhouse, smack on the riverbank, proved an ideal locale for my morning of reflection. This place, where we usually dived into the river as children, has remained unchanged. The tall marudam (*Terminalia arjuna*) trees on the banks, the sounds of a washerman beating clothes on a stone, a herd of cattle crossing the river in loose single file, the drumming call of the Crow-pheasant, a Pied kingfisher hovering purposefully over the water, the smell of hay and the azure blue sky dotted with just a few wispy tufts of cloud... It was as if time had stood still.

During my childhood, a holiday visit to the Amaravathi river with our little fox terrier Caesar in tow, was a daylong affair. With improvised tackles – fishhook tied to a string on a bamboo stick – we sometimes landed fish. There were days when we joined the man who went about poking the slush at the water's edge with a long pole to locate mud turtles. The pool of crystal-clear water, upstream in a dilapidated dam, was the venue for our water games, like catch-as-catch-can. This was where our seniors gave us swimming lessons.

Most of our waking hours were spent in the open. When we were not at school, we were either in the river or on top of the kudai seetha trees (*Acacia arabica*) that dotted the open landscape. With a flat, umbrella-like canopy and dark bark, this tree is typical of the dry, arid zone in the western part of Tamil Nadu. We were as much at home on the treetops as we were below. Neither the thorns among the leaves nor the occasional Bronze-keelback snake that showed up in the branches, swift as a lightning, deterred us. The games we played, like *udhiyangombu*, called for deft climbing of trees and adeptness at jumping down quickly. Often the girls joined us.

The night sky was full of stars and we could see the Milky Way clearly beyond. On moonlit nights, we stayed longer in the open and it was time for hide-and-seek. This game was very popular because it gave us a chance to huddle with girls under the cover of darkness. There was more seeking than hiding in this game. When I came home from college during my holidays, the girls had grown distant. You had to devise and play more complicated games in order to get anywhere close.

My work took me to different parts of India. Wherever we lived, our annual trip to my village acquired the dimensions of a pilgrimage. For our children, a visit to the river, along with the ride in the jutka that took us there, was often the high point of their holidays. They would romp noisily in the shallow waters and ask me to catch the tiny fish that darted past their feet in the gin-clear water.

In those years, when lethal pesticides and weedicides were unknown, the river was a habitat for myriad life forms. In the marudam trees that flank the river roosted hundreds of flying foxes. On many days, we have watched these nocturnal creatures set out at dusk to feed on fruits. In spots undisturbed by humans, such as the Thoovanam, otters frolicked in the water. In forested areas such as Kallapuram, elephants, gaur and sambar picked their way through the trees towards dusk for a drink of water. Tigers preyed on deer and guarded their territory. The river sustained an impressive variety of fish. From our village market, we bought carp, catfish, eels and fresh-water prawns. The reeds along the bank were home to bitterns and White-breasted water hens. At least three species of kingfishers could be seen: the white-breasted, the pied and the common. Hordes of birds came to drink, to bathe or to feed.

In the evening I was by the river again. Coconut trees stood silhouetted against a low, crimson sky. A flock of sandqrouse arrived at the water's edge for a last drink. In the light of the setting sun, the thin strands of the river appeared like molten gold. On my left, in the fading light, I saw a stretch of sand in front of the Thillaburi Amman temple. This was where we had gathered the day after Gandhiji's assassination to listen to speeches and sing songs at a memorial meeting. My memory of that evening is a picture of our music teacher, Devadas vathiyar, leaning on the wheels of a cart and wailing.

In the Tamil month of Adi (August) there are freshes in the river and people welcome it by celebrating the water festival *Adi pathinettu*. On the 18th of the month, the whole village comes to the riverbanks bearing mud plates of sprouted greengrams and rice which are dropped into the river. Community cooking on the riverbank culminates in a feast. The boys indulge in daring water sports like jumping into the swirling waters from the bridge.

But Amaravathi, once a perennial river, fed by the southwest and northeast monsoon, went completely dry for the first time in history, in 2002. It was a heart-rending sight: a desolate stretch of sand bereft of any sign of life. The widespread clearing of forests that clothed the mountains at the headwaters of the river is the main cause. Along its course, the riverine forests that flourished on the banks have also been cleared, drying up all the springs. The damming of the Amaravathi and some of its tributaries like Uppar upstream have also contributed to this calamity. In many places, an exotic species of Prosopis (*Prosopis juliflora*) is growing on the bed of the river, creating islands that are spreading inexorably.

Leaving Dharapuram behind, the Amaravathi takes a sharp bend, follows a winding course and meanders towards Karur. There are references to Karur and to the river in *Ahananooru* poems of Sangam anthology and the Tamil epic *Silapathikaram*. This town, mentioned by Ptolemy as a flourishing trading post in ancient times, has now been identified with Vanji of the Chera kingdom. Hordes of Roman coins have been unearthed from the riverbed. In 1997, a cache of jewels was recovered from the riverbed during a surface exploration. The finds included a golden ring, with a couple depicted in relief, attributed to second century BC. A few kilometres downstream, near Kattalai the Amaravathi merges with the Kaveri. As it approaches the sea, the Kaveri flows into a maze of channels. There the waters blend into the Bay of Bengal and with the oceans beyond.

–

The Hindu
(25.06.2000)

Saving The Treasured Islands

Roll on, thou deep and dark Blue oceans – roll
Man marks Earth with ruin – his control
Stops with the shore.

-Byron

If Byron were to visit the Andaman and Nicobar Islands today, he would be proved wrong. He wrote these lines long before Rachel Carson pointed out in her book *The Sea Around Us* (1951) how humans have ruined the oceans and the creatures sustained by them.

Andaman and Nicobar Islands are a continuation of the Arakan-Yoma mountain ranges of Myanmar. When the sea level rose 50,000 years ago, the land connections were cut off and the elevated areas emerged as islands. The rain forests of these islands, covering from the very edge of the water to the hilltops, suggest timelessness. The variety of life forms they support is matched by very few places in the rest of the world. So are the coral reefs and the marine waters here. Corals, fish, mollusks and sea grass – the incredible biodiversity of the coral reefs have earned them the name "underwater rain forests".

The remoteness and isolation of these islands shape new species of plants and animals and endow the islanders with distinct characteristics. [On island ecology, see *The Song of the Dodo* by David Quammem (1997).] There are seventeen birds unique to the islands, including the fabled Nicobar pigeon. Among mammals, you have the Crab-eating macaque and the Andaman wild pig. Along with 221 flowering plants, the famous Padauk tree, which provided timber to the mainland for many years, is exclusive to these islands. The sea around the islands is home to creatures like the rare dugong, dolphins, whales and turtles and nearly 200 species of corals. Considering the wealth of wildlife here, the government has created nearly 100 sanctuaries and nine national parks. The sea has been a great protection to the islands and its creatures.

But the natural heritage of these islands is threatened. The incredible wealth of biodiversity – of these 349 islands and the waters surrounding them – is in danger. As it was a penal settlement, the British did not pay much attention to its natural wealth. After colonizers arrived in the middle of 19th century, timber, matchwood, paper and plywood industries ravaged the jungles. Settlers cleared primeval forests. Trawler fishing took its toll. A trawler is to sea as what a bulldozer is to rain forests. It cleans up the sea floor. The dense evergreen forest mangrove tracts, products of a million years, can never be recreated. Development and mounting human pressure endanger the future of this precious ecosystem. The relict population of indigenous people of the islands also faces new threats.

It was in this backdrop that a group of concerned Foresters, ecologists, activists from non-governmental organizations and scientists got together in July 2000 in Port Blair to look at the status of the wildlife of Andamans and to consider ways of protecting the biodiversity. The Forest Department of A&N administration, the Fauna and Flora International and the Darwin Initiative jointly sponsored the workshop.

The workshop's participants were concerned that some major questions are being given short shrift. How do we create space for people's participation in conservation planning? How to stem human pressure? How do we dispose garbage? How do you protect the indigenous people? How far can tourism be permitted? What is the safe limit? Should chartered flights be allowed to bring in tourist hordes? For instance, boats carrying visitors to the islands, drop anchor at various points and the corals get destroyed. This has happened in the last few years. The edible swiftlet nest is robbed as it fetches fabulous prices in the East. Pirates and poaching gangs hover around.

Sashank, a scuba diver researching on corals, said that the shark population has declined steeply. He rarely sees them now. Ravi Shankar, who had stayed for a month in the uninhabited island of Norcondam to study the endemic hornbills, highlighted the devastation caused by stray dogs and feral cats and pleaded for eradication of all introduced species. Four varieties of sea turtles, including the rare and the largest, the Leatherback, come to lay eggs in the 1912 kilometre coastline of the archipelago. Stray dogs dig up turtle' nests to feed on the eggs. (This is happening in Chennai beaches also.) As there are no original predators in the islands, the creatures here are not equipped to escape should one appear on the scene. Feral cats feed on nestlings of various birds and also on lizards. The chital, introduced here decades back, is retarding the growth of forests. How can we encounter these threats?

The workshop also discussed the draft Biological Diversity Bill that envisages setting up the National Biodiversity Authority. Not just in the Andaman archipelago, but elsewhere in India also, we have areas where certain species are concentrated and are endemic to the area. The Nilgiri tahr in the Western Ghats is one such example. The bill aims to facilitate protection of the habitats of such creatures.

On the last day we were in Grubb Island, a patch of primeval forest, surrounded by white coral sand, gin clear water. In the blue sky overhead, two White-bellied sea eagles sailed majestically; it was magical. I waded into the lagoon carrying little Shavini, child of one of the participants. As she shrieked with glee and hit the water with both hands, I wondered what kind of a world we would leave for her generation.

–

The Hindu
(02.06.2002)

ONE EARLY MORNING IN TAMBARAM

I try not to miss any opportunity to stay overnight in the campus of Madras Christian College, Tambaram. It is not the mere prospect of a nostalgic trip in the alma mater, but the early morning stroll in the wooded campus is so full of possibilities.

The Church of Scotland missionaries who founded this college soon realized that it had outgrown its premises in George Town. When the first sod was turned in 1932 at the new site in Tambaram, the 370 acres area was quite barren. Edward Barnes, who was supervising the construction, was keen on trees and plants. He not only oversaw the construction; with the help of his wife Alice, he ensured that a jungle came up in the campus. Even as he planted trees, he collected plant specimens for Kew Gardens, London. In 1937, Governor Lord Erskine inaugurated the new building.

In a few undisturbed decades, a scrub jungle with all its characteristic denizens came up. Now it is home to a cross section of wildlife of this part of the country. Some exotic trees – Tabebuia, Copperpod and Gulmohar – were also planted along the avenues. In my student days, the carpet of yellow flowers under the Copperpod trees in March was a grim reminder of the impending examinations.

At the Guest house, I woke up to the song of a Magpie Robin that was holding a predawn concert of varied, fluid notes. We set out quite early. After a downpour, a scrub jungle brims with activity. Winged termites were emerging; drongos and babblers were there, ready to feast on them. Blood-red velvet mites could be spotted on the ground inching their way along. Though we did not sight, we heard the call of a distant peacock. This seems to be a recent addition. Soon koels started calling, with an occasional Tree pie joining in. The small lake on the eastern corner of the campus, that attracts dabchicks, White-breasted waterhen and coots after the monsoon, was dry.

As the sun came up, we could spot a variety of butterflies. A few years ago, Ruth Paulraj, a school student from Kodaikanal, studying the butterflies of the campus, logged 85 species, including the Black Rajah. The rare Moon moth has been recorded here. Two bushes of Kaya flower were in bloom, in brilliant heliotrope colour. Of the myriads of wildflowers here the most striking is the Glory lily or *kanthazh*, the state flower of Tamil Nadu. It is a twiner with deep orange flowers of six narrow petals. Mentioned in Sangam poems, the flower has been compared to lanterns and broken bangles. One poet says that a woman's fingers, by constant kneading of curds, was soft as a *Kanthazh* flower.

One of the memories of my college days is walking behind Dr. Kibble in a bridle path through the bushes on a birding trip. Later, Dr. Gift Siromoney, following the eccentric Scot, studied the birds of the campus and published a checklist with more than 96 species, including the fabled Paradise flycatcher. Siromoney has written quite a few scientific papers on the natural history of the campus.

This small patch of wilderness hosts an impressive list of mammals. The most visible are the Chital, recent migrants from the adjacent reserve forest. But they already pose a problem by the pressure they exert on the plants. When the Air force station bordering the college faced a similar problem, they organized a drive in 1997 and through a specially erected corridor, flushed about 200 chital into the Vandalur zoo compound.

Toddy cats have been sighted. They probably find shelter in the Palmyra trees on the eastern end of the campus. The sightings of two animals recently have been noted with enthusiasm by wildlifers: Porcupine and Pangolin or the Scaly Anteater, both endangered. In most of its home range, Pangolin is all but gone. Porcupine was spotted by Job Thomas, a professor visiting from the US. When I went looking one night along with the professor, the animals decided to remain hidden. There is even a record of sighting a leopard cat here in the fifties.

Mongoose and monitor lizards show up easily. I recall how one morning, when I was a resident in St. Thomas hall, two monitors were engaged in a fight in front of the entrance, and a small crowd had gathered around to cheer them. The lizards, rearing on their hind legs and trying to get a hold on each other like two Sumo wrestlers, were so engrossed in the bout that it took a while before they realized that they had drawn spectators and scurry into the undergrowth.

The students have now formed an outfit, the Scrub Society, which came into being quite accidentally. In 1989, the college was planning a national fair on water management. For this purpose, ironically, eleven acres of forest was cleared. A group of students, calling themselves the Green Freaks, protested vehemently and stopped further damage. The Scrub Society came into being. Run by students, this society has a number of activities such as turtle walks and an annual event, Deep Woods, to spread environmental awareness.

In 2002, the Chennai-based NGO for trees Nizhal organized a memorable walk around the campus, led by Dr. Narasimhan, professor of Botany. A Vagai tree was pointed out to us. The kings of ancient days sported a garland of Vagai flowers, much like the olive wreath of Romans, when they won a battle (hence the Tamil phrase *vagai soodiya*). There was an Athondai creeper, which has lent its name to Thondai nadu, the medieval name for Chengalpattu area. We were shown Red sanders tree, an endemic, and also a rare Fern tree. The unusually tall banyan in front of the guest houses is so majestic that you understand why this tree often takes on a religious aura. There are quite a few peepul and neem trees, which are also associated with worship. The walk ended under a tree where a colony of fruit bats was roosting.

While forests are disappearing fast all over, there are these precious little patches in cities, like the Jawaharlal Nehru University campus in Delhi, the Hyderabad Central University and Madras IIT. The MCC campus is one such oasis in an urban desert and needs to be managed carefully. One thing that strikes a visitor is Ventilago creepers choking smaller trees. This has to be addressed. The deer problem is there to be tackled. Because there are too many of them, the deer keep the forest from regenerating. This campus with its wildlife is a priceless heritage and has to be saved. It is an obligation the college has to the rest of the world.

–

Madras Musings
(May 2013)

Banyans and Baobabs: The Trees of Chennai

As the plane banked deeply and aligned itself to land, I could get a good view of the city of Chennai. Though, from the air, it appears to be a city of trees, much of the tree cover has gone, replaced by buildings and roads. When the British traders landed and established Fort St. George, sowing the seed for the city of Madras, the area was covered with scrub jungle, lakes and lagoons. In the course of the past three hundred years, the landscape has changed, leaving a representative selection of the original flora at the Guindy National Park around the Raj Bhavan. You can see rows of Palmyra palms there.

The evergreen indigenous trees like the banyan, peepul, neem, mango, pungamia, tamarind and wood apple can be seen in some parts of the city. In recent decades, we observe a change in the kind of trees that are planted. Exotics, which are small in spread and weak in trunk, are planted widely. There is a need to propagate indigenous varieties such as neem and peepul.

However, there are many pockets of vegetation in private properties of Chennai in which some of the original landscapes have been preserved, along with the trees and shrubs native to this soil. One is the campus of the Madras Christian College in Tambaram, there are quite a few records of its flora and fauna. An idea of the wealth of plant life in Chennai area can be had from the fact that in this

370 acres campus, 120 varieties of trees and 600 varieties of plants have been identified. Many of these species can be seen in the campus of the Indian Institute of Technology which is an extension of the Guindy National Park, and Theosophical Society also. The other places of botanical wealth in the city are the Government estate in Anna Salai, the Agri-Horticulture Society compound and the campus of the YMCA college of Physical Education.

There are many trees and plants in the city that have been mentioned in ancient Tamil lexicons called *Nigandu* (2nd AD). For instance, *Pingala Nigandu* lists a number of trees, many of which can still be sighted in the city. The Indian Laburnum (*Cassia fistula*) is the konrai of the lexicon era. It blossoms into clusters of bright yellow flowers in summer and has long dark cylindrical pods. Another tree mentioned in ancient texts is kumizhi, which has been identified as *Gmelina arborea*, a large tree that bears yellow globular fruits. This tree, still found in Chennai area, was used to make musical instruments such as the yazh, a stringed device.

The poets of the Sangam period (3rd AD to 6th AD) were tuned to Nature and their writings are replete with references to trees and flowers. Scholars who have identified most of the plants and trees mentioned by these poets point out that there are many instances where the modern nomenclature of these plants can be traced to Sangam poetry. P. L. Swamy has identified all the 99 plants mentioned in the poetical work *Kurinjipattu*.

Another tree well known to ancient Tamils is vengai (*Pterocarpus marsupium*) with its bright yellow flowers. These trees can be easily spotted in the Guindy National Park and also in Vandalur hills in the outskirts of the city. The word vengai also stands for tiger in Tamil. The yellow flowers that fall from the tree on the dark background of the forest floor appear like the colour of the tiger. There is a poem which talks about an elephant charging a vengai tree, mistaking it for a tiger. The vengai tree was widely used for furniture making during the British period.

The most majestic of all Chennai trees is the Banyan (*Ficus bengalensis*), famous for its aerial roots and its uses in Indian medicine. When it is in fruition a variety of birds come to feed on them. Evidently there were hundreds of these trees in Chennai. Inside the campus of the Indian Institute of Technology in Guindy there are at least 200 banyan trees. Old photographs of Mowbray's Road (present TTK Salai) show large banyan trees flanking it. The banyan at the Theosophical Society in Adyar, a huge sprawling tree with its hundreds of aerial roots, was one of the tourist attractions till a cyclonic storm brought it down in 1983. But the tree has been revived through the aerial roots. Another legendary indigenous tree of Chennai is the Kadamba (*Barringtonia acutangula*). This tree, found in large numbers, half submerged in water in Vedanthangal, serves as nesting site for thousands of waterfowl every year. Its flowers are associated with the worship of Murugan. There is a village near Chennai called Kadaperi, which means "lake of Kadamba tree". The neem, another common tree of the city, is much used in indigenous medicine, particularly its oil and leaves. Its oilcake is used as a fertilizer. The Adyar estuary was once home to a stretch of mangrove forest. After the degradation of the estuary, only a remnant of the once luxurious growth is seen.

Three well-known varieties of palm trees are found within the city: the Coconut (*Coco nucifera*), the Palmyra (*Brasses flabelliform)* and the Wild date palm (*Phoenix Sylvester's*). The coconut is particularly very popular and each house plot has its share of coconut palms. Like the Palmyra, the wild date palm is also an indigenous tree. One of the most picturesque trees is the Talipot palm (*Corypha macropoda*); this name is a modified version of its indigenous name *Thazhipanai.* One of the tallest palms of the world, it can grow up to 25 metres. This tree blossoms only once in its lifetime, after which it dies. Referred to as a monocarp by botanists, this tree sports its blossom for three months. The flowers burst forth on the top of the tree like frozen fireworks. There was a tree just outside the Pallavaram railway station on the hillside. There were two specimens inside the campus of the Madras Christian College.

With the coming of the colonizers, a large number of trees were brought in from other lands, from the Americas on this side and from Australia on the other, and planted as avenue trees. These immigrants have almost taken over the city and you see them along the main roads. The most popular among these is the Gulmohur (*Delonix regia*) with brilliant red flowers that almost replaces the green foliage of the tree. A native of Madagascar, this is grown easily, so it soon became a popular avenue tree. The Tulip tree (*Spathodia companulata*), with its large red flowers, is indigenous to East Africa and has been successfully introduced in India. This tall evergreen is often mistaken for the Flame of the forest of our forests. Another tree found in campuses such as the Madras Museum is the Rusty Shieldbearer (*Peltophoum inerme*), that bears a profusion of bright yellow flowers in summer. Another avenue tree, seen in many roads of Chennai, including the Raj Bhavan road, bears bright yellow flowers in summer is *Peltophorum ferrugineum*, a native of Malaysia. The fallen flowers of this tree carpet the ground below and strike a beautiful picture. Another exotic flowering tree is *Mimosops elongi,* a native of Siam. *Tabebuia rosea,* a Mexican tree, has been planted widely and can be seen in the campuses of Anna University and Madras University.

The Rain tree (*Enterolobium saman*) is another prominent exotic in Chennai planted extensively as avenue trees. Old and large specimens can be seen inside many private compounds and government properties such as the Madras Museum compound. A native of Central America and West Indies, it has a vast, spreading crown. It is so named from the presence of moisture on the ground under the tree. One exotic that seem to have taken over the city is *Prosopis juliflora*, found in abundance along the riverbanks and in vacant plots inside the city. It is often used as firewood.

The most picturesque of all exotic trees is the Baobab (*Adansonia digitata*) or Monkey-bread tree. For reasons I am not able to figure out, it is locally referred to as Papara *puliamaram*. A native of Africa, this tree was introduced in India by the Arabs. It is a giant deciduous tree with a smooth, bottle shaped trunk. Its gourds are used as floats in Gujarat. Good specimens of this tree can be seen in the Theosophical society campus. Near the auditorium of the Madras Medical College also is a well grown baobab.

One dimension of our colonial heritage, exotic trees are not without problems. For instance, the Gulmohar sheds its leaves in summer, when we most need shade. The alien trees are not as strong as native species which have evolved in this climate and soil. In 2016 about 200 large avenues trees in the city were uprooted by a storm, all of them exotics. There is a need to promote indigenous trees.

In the last few years, there have been sporadic attempts at greening the city. In 1999, the Green Belt for Abatement of Pollution Scheme was launched and tree wardens were nominated in different areas of the city. But the scheme was soon forgotten along with the tree wardens. The Urban Forestry Wing in the Chennai Corporation was created in 2002. One of its aims is to bring in an Urban Tree Protection Act, on the lines of Karnataka and Andhra. The act would cover all trees, in public and private areas, within the city. But it is yet to make its appearance. The non-governmental initiative has been encouraging. In 2005, Nizhal, (meaning Shade) was founded to promote tree culture.

The public obsession with coconut palms militates against providing a proper green cover. Though hardly anyone harvests coconuts from the trees planted in their houses, the tree remains popular. The concretizing pavements have spelt death for the trees. The tree trunk is covered all around, as if it is a lamp post and eventually it dies. There has been no sustained tree-growing programme in the city.

–

The Hindu

(11.03.2008)

The lost orchid *Paphilopedilum drury*

Chestnet tailed starling

Flamingos in Adyar estuary

Teacher and his students in a village near Bandipur.

Kurinji Flower

Kombai Breed

Wild Dogs

Moniter Lizards

Pangolin

Banyan tree in Guindy Naational Park

Baobob tree in The Theosophical Society

Personalities

The Noah's Ark Method In Conservation

Born in Jamshedpur, Gerald Durrell founded his own zoo in 1958 on a forty-acre area in the little village of Trinity, Jersey, in Channel Islands, England. The purpose was to breed endangered animals in captivity and thus save them from extinction. Durrel was in Shillong, Meghalaya in 1978 to study the Pygmy hog and White-winged wood duck, both endangered species. He spoke on the hazards of tampering with the ecosystem.

Question : On what criteria do you select animals to be bred in captivity?

When a species gets below a certain level in numbers in the wild state, then you know it needs captive breeding. For example, the Pink pigeons of Mauritius are down to 35 or 38 birds. If there is a bad cyclone in Mauritius, the Pink pigeons would be finished. So we have set up a captive breeding colony in Mauritius and we have one in Jersey. What we are trying to do in Jersey is simply to build up colonies of such species. I had a telegram recently from Jersey that a Pink pigeon in our colony has just laid two eggs.

Q. How do you tackle the problem of raising species from totally different climatic zones in your zoo at Jersey? For instance, you have African Servel and many creatures from Madagascar.

We manage to acclimatize them. It is a slow process. Sometimes it takes three years. We have marmosets from Brazil which couldn't be better. They have been provided with heated indoor quarters, bedrooms with infrared lights and an open enclosure into which they can go even in snow. But they can always get back to the heated room to warm themselves. It is exactly like human beings. You live in Shillong. You go for a walk and it's cold outside. You come in and light a fire. There is a lot of nonsense talked about adaptation of animals to cold climates. Look at the variety of climates we have adapted ourselves to from the tropics right up to the frozen north… the Gobi desert, the Belgian Congo… You name it, we have adapted ourselves. We can do exactly the same thing with animals, if we do it cautiously.

Q. To be bred at Jersey you choose small and rare animals, usually neglected by conservationists. The data available on their behaviour pattern and diet requirements are meagre. How do you manage to breed them?

There is a saying in England: If a farmer sows and all the crops come up well, we say, "He has green fingers." I suppose we have green fingers for animals. But it is all trial and error… experimentation and watching the animals closely. The animals are, so to speak, under a microscope, all the time so that every detail is observed. An animal may be in perfect shape, eating well and so forth, but may not breed. And then you may hit upon some tiny point that will make all the difference and that may make the animal to breed.

Q. You should have the habitat to release the animals bred in captivity. How effective can captive breeding be when the habitat is being destroyed so fast all over the world?

Yes, this is a grave problem. The destruction is so rapid and the conservation movement is not quite catching up with it. All that one can do is to keep the animals in captivity – at least we will know that they are safe there – while at the same time try to preserve the habitat. While you should never lose sight of the fact that the preservation of the habitat is all important, not as important from the animals' point of view as it is from ours. Because if we go on destroying the habitats at the rate we do, we are simply committing suicide. It is as simple as that.

Q. Has the Jersey wildlife Preservation Trust been able to reintroduce any species that has been bred there in captivity?

No, not yet. But we have a number of species to be reintroduced in their original homes if we can have safe areas to do so. For example, we have 120 White-eared pheasants, all bred from the original four pairs I got from China. It is a dual thing. While trying to preserve them in captivity, we fight the whole way to preserve the habitat. But it is an uphill struggle.

Q. Has your work, that is your zoo at Jersey, influenced the thinking in other zoos? For instance, has the Zoo Directors' Union been receptive to your ideas?

I think so. They now come to us for advice, for help. Not because I am clever. If I am clever at all, I am so in choosing the right people to do the job. And I have a very good team of dedicated workers. You know the old saying, "If you make good mouse-traps, people will beat a path to your door even if you do it in the middle of the jungle." For this is what a zoo should be doing, not a mere place of amusement which is what the majority of zoos are.

Q. Have you got any animal from India for breeding at Jersey?

Not right now, but we hope to get a pair of Pygmy hogs from Zurich zoo.

Q. You were interested in spotting the rare white-winged wood duck in Assam. Were you able to?

Yes. This was near a tea garden in Goalpara. We spotted them in their original habitat on the banks of the river. We could not see anything on our first evening. The next day we saw them in flight. It was a magnificent sight.

Q. You have visited Assam, the richest area in the country in terms of wildlife. What impression do you carry back?

I was tremendously impressed with Manas and Kaziranga sanctuaries. People should not think that conservation is a fad. Conservation is really the preservation of the world we are living in. The way forest wealth is being destroyed all over the world is horrifying. Over a period of years, this will alter the climate, create flash floods, take away the top soil, then desert areas will come into being. We are still so ignorant of how the world works. We are really like children trying to mend a watch with a hammer. Take this effort at planting Brazil nut trees in the farms in Brazil. They grew well but didn't bear any fruit. The reason was that the flower of the Brazil nut tree is like a little cup with a lid and there is only one species of bee which feeds on these flowers and pollinates them. They would not go into the farm as there were no other trees to feed on once they were finished with the few Brazil nut trees. Now they plant one row of Brazil nut trees and three or four rows of other flowering trees and the farming has been successful.

–

The Hindu

(30.04.1978)

The Bite Of A Snake

Romulus Whitaker, *India's leading herpetologist, has been doing a survey of snakebite incidence in India. He points out that there are basically four venomous snakes that figure in snakebite cases: cobra, Russell's viper, saw scaled viper and krait. He calls them the Big Four. He was conferred the Padma Sri in 2018.*

–

Q. How did this idea of a survey begin?

It began as an idea to make a film on snakebite in India. When I started serious filmmaking in 1986, our first film was "Snakebite". After seventeen years, I thought it would be a good idea to go back to the subject. We traveled to areas in Tamil Nadu, Kerala, Rajasthan and West Bengal where incidence of snakebite is high, to specific areas, where different snakes are responsible for the bites. In Rajasthan it was all Saw-scaled viper. In northern Kerala it was mainly bites of Russell's viper and down here in Tamil Nadu it is a mixture of cobras and kraits. In Bengal it was a mix of all of the Big Four venomous snakes, except the saw scaled viper.

Q. How serious a problem is snakebite in India?

The truth is that compared to many infectious diseases that kill people like simple diarrhea, the 15,000 to 20,000 deaths by snakebite each year is not one of the really big medical issues in India. In fact, statistics indicate you are twice as likely to die of rabies in India than by snakebite. To me that's very scary! But snakebite is also a traumatic experience that many in the villages think more about it than about other diseases. It is still surrounded by such mystery and is frequently associated with gods and devils.

An international expert on snakebite, the late Dr. Alistair Reid of the Liverpool School of Tropical Medicine, found that only 10 to 15% of venomous bites end in death. The possibility of survival, even without treatment, is incredibly good. There are many reasons for this. One is that snakes often administer dry bites. That is, the snake does not always inject venom. Sometimes, they might inject only a tiny bit of venom. The snake can inject the quantity of venom it wants. This is an entirely voluntary process. This I learnt by doing thousands of venom extractions. Sometimes the snake will not give any venom at all. But you never know how much venom was injected into you except by the progress of the symptoms.

Q. Do we have reliable data on snakebite?

Actually we do not really have up-to-date data, as the statistics are not very clear or simply absent. But the latest survey we have was done in 1972 by Dr. Sawai and Dr. Homma of the Japan Snake Institute. They selected about ten hospitals in India and estimated how many came to hospital after snakebite, how many died there and also estimates of how many died outside the hospitals. This latter, of course, could only be conjecture. The report concluded that about 10% of deaths are of victims who come to the hospital and about 90% die outside, having gone for other remedies like mantra, magic, stationmaster and so on. It is very different now, after thirty years.

Based on this recent preliminary survey that Janaki and I did in Kerala, West Bengal and Rajasthan, we found that the awareness about anti-venom serum is much higher now than 1972. Most doctors think that a majority of snakebite victims now come to hospitals (often after wasting time on a village remedy). They think that the death rate might have reduced greatly. What we do not know is whether the actual incidence of snakebite is increasing. Let me explain this. By destroying forests and by creating agricultural land, we are increasing the prey base of the snake, that is frogs and rats. Basically I am talking about rice fields, which harbour millions of rats and so attract a lot of snakes. The number of snakes per acre in a rice field is abnormal compared to the natural population in the forest. So here you have humans going into the field every morning and coming out in the evening, just during the times when snakes are active. Thus the chance of an encounter between farmer and snake is very high. As more areas are inhabited at the peripheries of towns, even there, the chances of human/ snake interaction increase.

Q. Which snakebite is most common in India?

This varies from region to region. Wherever one species is more common and the chances of humans coming into contact is higher, the bite of that snake will occur more there. In Maharashtra, the Saw-Scaled viper is in plenty along the coast, so the vast majority of snakebites are from this species. In parts of North Kerala, near Kannur area, Russell's viper is very common, so most of the bites there are from this snake. We found in parts of Bengal also, Russell's viper is very common. In a place like this (Chingleput district of Tamil Nadu) cobra bites are more common merely because this area abounds in that snake. So this issue is very region-specific. This pattern tends to change also. One doctor in Bengal who had handled about 30,000 snakes bites told us that over the years, Russell's viper bites are getting more common than cobra bites due to as-yet unknown ecological reasons.

Q. Do you observe any increase in the awareness on snakebites and the need for prompt treatment?

Based on the statistics we got from the Pappinisseri Visha Chikitsa Centre (Pappinisseri Venom Centre in Kerala), where they have treated 48000 snakes bites, the details show that non-venomous snakes had bitten more than half the victims who came. But all patients who come are subject to observation. This shows increasing awareness on snakebite and the need to get antivenom serum treatment. When we visited this centre, I pointed out the possibility of dry bites by venomous snakes. However, I still think that we have a long way to go to raise awareness on this issue, especially in less literate parts of the country.

Q. What is the percentage of venomous snakebites that go untreated in your opinion?

It is very difficult to say. A cobra bite, a Russell's viper bite and Saw -scaled viper bite all have different symptoms. Krait bite is much less obvious, and it is very difficult for people to know that they have been bitten at all. There may be no pain and no symptoms to be alarmed at, so people may not take it seriously and go to hospital, especially in the middle of the night when most of such bites occur. So unfortunately Krait bite is more often fatal than bites from the other three of the Big Four.

Q. Is it correct to say that if a snake has bitten in the recent past, its poison is less in the subsequent bite?

No. A snake never runs out of venom and it does not inject all the venom from the sac. Those of us who have been extracting venom know this well.

Q. Recently it has been found that what were considered sub species among cobras in various parts of India are in fact separate species. Does this have implications on production of anti-venom?

The word is still not in on this issue as the research is not yet complete in this area. But certainly this raises new problems. The big question being: Will anti-venom made from the venom of one species effectively neutralize another? It was found that anti-venom made from the Indian Russell's viper is not too effective for Russell's viper bite in Sri Lanka. Venom variation is an interesting but unstudied subject. In India we have three species of cobras: the spectacled cobra, the monocled cobra, which is in the Northeast, and the black cobra, which is way up in the Northwest.

Q. What about the production of anti-venom in India?

Production is not adequate. And certainly in rural areas, its distribution is not adequate, though it is much better than what it was. The other day, a Russell's viper bit a farmhand near our house as he was trying to catch a monitor lizard. He was taken to a Tirukazhukunram clinic and treated. If you combine increasing quantity with availability and also awareness, there will be far fewer deaths due to snakebites. Anti-venom, when lyophilized, does not need refrigeration and can keep for five years. So we should have all Primary Health Centres stocking anti-venom

Q. Is dialysis resorted to as a treatment for snakebite?

Yes. The typical systemic reaction to a serious bite of Russell's viper is kidney breakdown. At that stage, dialysis is essential to pull a victim through.

Q. Have you come across any case in which a known venomous snakebite has been countered by traditional medicine?

Firstly, much snakebite is by non-venomous snakes. Secondly, a large percentage of venomous snakebites are dry bites. A cobra once bit me and it was a dry bite. I did not develop any symptom of a cobra bite. We know that at least 80 to 90% survival is guaranteed without any treatment. With that sort of success rate to any healer, be it herbal, "snakestone" or mantra, or plain soda water, most villagers would be happy to go to him, though he is a potential serial killer. If he lost even one patient, he is a murderer. He may be successful with other ailments like fever, common cold and whatever. But in snakebite, you are looking at a person who is lying on the operating table, as it were, with his body cut open. I mean, it's equivalent to that. And he has to be in the hands of someone who can deal with that. A man who supplies some local medicine cannot handle it. The Irulas, the traditional snake catchers with their own sophisticated herbal medicine system, have now understood the position. They know that the snake gives an injection and the venom goes deep into your system and this can be neutralized only by a similar injection, not by oral or locally applied remedies, no matter how famous.

Q. What is the status of venomous snakes in India?

Cobras flourish as long as there are rice fields; there they feed mainly on the mole rat (*varapu eli* in Tamil), live and lay their eggs in the rat burrow networks. Kraits also get by very well in rice fields because they like the plentiful small rodents such as the field mouse (*sundeli*) and rock mouse (*kallu eli*). We have found a lot of kraits in the mounds of earth and rubble near wells. Russell's vipers live in the rocky outcrops and hedgerows of cactus and other bush which often form the boundaries of agricultural land. There, on the high ground, they have a plentiful supply of common gerbil (*velleli*) which are also attracted to the wealth of food humans provide by their farming activities! But thanks to snakes, we are not overrun by rodents (yet)!

–

The Hindu
(13.06.2004)

Salvaging The Rain Forest

The drumming calls of the Nilgiri langur came floating through the dense canopy like a secret code of the denizens of the forests. The shrill calls of cicadas that pervaded the forest rose up to a crescendo and stopped abruptly, only to begin again tentatively a few seconds later. We gingerly picked our way along a damp bridle path. This is one of the last redoubts of rain forests in the Western Ghats and I was with a team of youngsters who believed that this pristine heritage could be saved.

Divya Muddappa and Shankararaman, wildlife biologists stationed in the tea town of Valparai in Tamil Nadu, were engaged in a bid to restore a few degraded rain forests patches to their natural state. After her doctoral studies, Divya came to this part of the Western Ghats to study the lesser-known carnivores of this area and Shankararaman chose this place to look at the elephant-human conflict. During their work, they observed that rain forests were very fragmented in this part of the Western Ghats and that certain patches of rain forest were degraded. They asked themselves if they could do anything to restore them to the original state during their stay in Valparai. Thus was born the Rain Forest Research and Restoration project under the aegis of Mysore-based The Nature Conservation Foundation.

What is a rain forest? Among the most ancient forests of the world, they are also the world's most endangered environment. Lying stretched on both sides of the Equator, between the tropics of Cancer and Capricorn, they are incredibly rich in biodiversity, both plants and animals, more than any other terrestrial eco system. The rain forests in Western Ghats are referred to as Shola forests, a take-off from the Tamil term *Solai*. It is important that we save this biodiversity treasure trove because it offers limitless opportunities for humankind. In Annamalai rainforest, you see a wild variety of rice and two kinds of wild bananas. Beyond Valparai, in the Annamalai ranges you still have breathtakingly beautiful forests. But unfortunately, most of the rain forests are in poor nations, so they are being chewed up at a fast rate.

The idea of this project came quite accidentally. While studying the carnivores in Kalakad forest near Tirunelveli, Divya was examining the scat of Civet cat and found some seeds in it. She wondered if they would germinate. They did, and she raised some saplings. After she moved to Valparai, she came up with this project for regeneration. The plan was simple. Collect the seeds from the forest, raise saplings, plant them in the degraded rainforest patches and see if they could heal the scars of logging. The Netherlands Committee for the International Union for Conservation of Nature came forward to fund this project under their Tropical Rainforest Programme.

In their quest to save rain forests, these young scientists won the goodwill of planters. In recent years, there has been a change in the planters' profile. The "huntin' shootin' fishing" planter has transformed into an ecologically sensitive manager and is active with the zeal of a new convert. They have formed the Annamalai Biodiversity Conservation Association to foster ecologically sound practices. Some of them, particularly, D. G. Hegde of Hindustan Lever, known for his pro-environment activities, offered support under his company's Sustainable Agriculture Project. An abandoned coffee curing yard at Injiparai was given to them to be used as a nursery and the scientists were permitted to work in some patches of rain forests within the estates.

While gathering seeds, they took care not to collect any from inside the rainforests but only from excrement of birds and animals and from roads, which would be lost in any case. For instance, a wild variety of Jamun seeds was gathered from scat of bears. Hornbills disperse certain varieties of seeds, so these were collected by these scientists from under the hornbills' nest. Giant squirrels disperse a certain variety of Leach seeds. In other words, they did not disturb the forest in any way.

Shankararaman pointed out that animals know where ripe fruits are found, so seeds from their scat will be of high quality. In Thailand, coffee seeds collected from civet cat excrement is highly valued by planters. To germinate the seeds, they gathered soils from the area where the seeds were found. This was mixed with sand and some compost. Chemical manure or pesticide was not used in this effort.

For this, they needed protected areas to plant the saplings raised. Divya and Shankararaman were given three sites in different levels of degradation, covering a total of 7500 square metres, where they could carry on their work. They started planting the saplings in 2002. Just in one site of the Hindustan Level tea estates, christened the Injiparai biodiversity plot, over 1800 saplings of 80 varieties of trees have been planted.

The seeds were collected and classified, sown in narrow beds and the tiny seedlings placed in polythene bags. To keep away squirrels and hares that have a partiality to seeds, the sheds in which the saplings were raised had been rodent-proofed. Before being planted in the protected area, the seedlings were put through a "hardening" process by exposing them to sunlight. The saplings were then planted in spots in areas not covered by any canopy.

All planting was done during monsoon period for higher success rates. Right from the seed collection stage, each sapling was tagged and monitored and the history of each sapling was meticulously documented. The team was happy with the progress.

The rain forest patches in which the saplings were placed were called 'Restoration plots' and now there are five such plots in Valparai. Saplings were planted in two plots in 2002 and in three in 2003. So far, 5000 saplings have been planted under the project and the Rain forest nursery now contains 20,000 saplings. Experimentally, some saplings have been planted in a patch of Eucalyptus plantation to check how they fare.

The significance of the Valparai experiment is that if proved successful, the insights gained in this effort could well point the way for rainforest restoration in other parts of the world.

–

(Recently a documentary titled **A Dream of Trees** on the work of these two sceintists have been released which points to the success of their experiment.)

The Hindu

(20.03.2004)

Western Ghats: Through The Viewfinder

The 59 black and white silver prints that make up "The Western Ghats: Portrait & Panorama" photographic exhibition at the India International Centre, New Delhi are designed to be both an educational and artistic experience. For Ian Lockwood, who teaches Environmental Science in a school in Colombo, this was the first major show in India. Critics are ecstatic about the exhibition.

I met Ian Lockwood recently in Chennai, just before he left for Delhi. The setting could not have been more appropriate; the farmhouse of herpetologist Romulus Whitaker, with a hill clothed in scrub-jungle forming the backdrop. As a Crimson-throated barbet kept up its drumming call, Ian talked about his childhood in Kodaikanal; it provided new paths to explore, streams to swim in, cliffs to climb and new ghat roads to cycle down. The several trips he made with family friends Romulus and Zai Whitaker left a marked influence on Ian's interest in natural history.

At some point in school he started carrying a small camera to document the places he saw. The parents were encouraging and tolerated him losing the camera, dunking another in a cold stream and wasting uncountable rolls of film. He used to spend afternoons hanging around the musty darkroom of Doveton's

Studio, the oldest photographic establishment in Kodak. The manager Rajkumar took him under his wing and showed how to use his darkroom. He encouraged Ian to record and interpret nature using black and white film, helping to develop it and make the prints. Photography soon became a passion for Ian.

Family was an important reason for his association with the landscape of South India and the Western Ghats. Grandfather Edson Lockwood had started hiking in the Palanis in the late 1920s. At a time when hunting was an acceptable activity, he was an amateur naturalist. Both Ian's mother and father attended boarding school in Kodaikanal in the 1950s, a time when the school was primarily composed of the children of American missionaries. Hiking was one of his father's favourite activities. When they lived in India in the early 1970s, he started documenting the mountainscapes around Kodaikanal.

The landscape of Western Ghats was breathtaking, but it was also changing. High altitude grasslands were disappearing as plantations of exotic trees were being rapidly introduced to the hills. The evergreen forests in lower valleys were being logged and there was steady environmental deterioration in the hills. When he was in the school, he noticed that the lake was being polluted, there was a noticeable increase in vehicular traffic and huge numbers of people thronged to the hills during season time. Encouraged by his father, Ian started to document the changing landscape in the 1990s. His motivating force was the hope that he could share the pictures with a wider audience to present a message of conservation and ecological awakening.

Ian's landscapes proclaim his relationship with Nature. You do not see any man-made object in his pictures. Rarely. There is nothing happening in his pictures. They document remote landscapes. When he was growing up in the Palani Hills, he couldn't help being awed by the grand cliffs, falling cascades, changing cloud patterns and deep forests that he was surrounded by. He spent weekends hiking and exploring the Palani Hills. He doodled mountain silhouettes in notebooks, wrote about magical moments in his diary, but photography became the best way for him to express these emotions. He believes that there should be a personal connection between the photographer and his or her subject matter, at least that is a good basis.

Lockwood says that he chooses to work in the black and white medium for two important reasons. Firstly, he prefers the emotional impact of black and white as an art form compared to colour. He believes that black and white pictures best convey the message and emotions that he visualizes and feels when he is interacting with Nature. It is his experience that the drama of the mountain scenery and the smaller details of the forest floor lend themselves best to black and white.

Secondly, black and white gives control over as much of the photographic process as possible and lends itself to this much more than colour (which, in a traditional sense, requires short lived, expensive chemistry). He takes the film from exposure all the way through development, printing and the final presentation of the exhibition print. He says he enjoys these controls over the final image, which were difficult with colour. Although digital photography has provided similar control, like many other photographers, he remains a disciple of what is called "straight" black & white photography. Perumal hills, Anaimudi Peak, the shola-grassland combination… all acquire an ethereal beauty through his camera.

Even to a casual viewer of the exhibition, the influence of legendary landscape photographer Ansel Adams is evident. The picture of Thalayar falls in the Palani hills is reminiscent of Adams' "Frozen lakes and Cliffs, Sequoia National Park". Ian says that this influence stems from his father, who introduced Adams' fine North American landscape work to Ian.

Ansel Adams had worked in large-format black and white. Moved by the incredible beauty of places like Yosemite, Adams had spent his life making classic images of Nature in the American West. He was significant in that he was one of the first photographers whose work was accepted as "art" by the suspicious artistic community in North America.

Also a perfectionist practitioner of straight photography, Adams knew his camera, how film worked, the workings of light and the photographic process like few others. This is encapsulated in the Zone System of exposure calculation that he co-developed to help photographers take images they had visualized in the field to the final print. He was also a tireless educator and crusader for the protection of the habitats that he photographed.

As Ian started to define his own photography, these attributes of Adams made him a perfect guru-type figure. (Adams himself had a guru, Alfred Stieglitz.) Sabastiao Salgado's black and white pictures of people in developing countries were also an influence on Ian.

Ian observed that there is an exciting situation for photography in India at the moment. India, of course, was one of the first countries to take to the new invention of photography in the mid-nineteenth century. Since that time, photography has spilt out into the media, arts, science, and corporate and natural history spheres of life in India. There are numerous Indian photographers who are well established. There are several magazines that publish articles on technique, equipment and the portfolios of different photographers. Several photographers have work that is accepted as "art" but much deserving work goes unnoticed in this field. This is an age dominated by computers, television and digital images. These tools have certainly challenged the conventional world of photography, but Ian does not see these developments as being life-threatening to photography in India. Photographers in India have to deal with the climatic challenges of living in a tropical country. High humidity and warm temperatures are not the ideal conditions to be shooting; processing and preserving photographs in. The storage of expensive equipment in humid areas is a major hindrance and all photographers have had to struggle with fungus on lenses. The varying seasons of South Asia offer some respite and it is not uncommon for photographers to be pursuing most of their work in the cool, relatively dry winter season!

Why did he choose to exhibit first in the capital? New Delhi is a long way from the Western Ghats, he said, yet the decisions made here influence what happens in these far-flung hills. With the proximity of the mighty Himalayas to New Delhi, it is easy to forget the majestic mountains of the Southern states.

The challenges to the Western Ghats are multi-faceted. Mining, dam building and the denotification of protected areas affects some areas, the continued introduction of exotic trees affect other habitats. The fragmentation of wildlife habitats and resulting loss of biodiversity is a serious threat. The selection of pictures was designed to give viewers a deeper understanding for the role that the Ghats play in water regulation for the plains as well as their significance as being one of India's most important locations for endemic biodiversity. Thankfully there are people working on different environmental and conservation issues in the Western Ghats. Some work with wildlife, others study vegetation issues, while some address the human elements in these fragile hills.

Lockwood photographs and shows it to people; He observed that, "I hope that people who see this exhibition will walk away with a new appreciation for the Western Ghats as a critical mountain region of India. I am interested in reaching the art, photographic and natural history communities, as well as anyone else with a curiosity for a remote part of this great country."

–

Frontline

(11.05.2001)

Saving The Tiger

Dr. Melvin E. Sunquist, professor of Wildlife Biology in the University of Florida, was the co-principal investigator in the tiger research conducted in Nagerhole sanctuary, Karnataka, in the nineteen-nineties. He was a pioneer in using radio-telemetry method to study tigers in Chitawan National park in Nepal. The project in Nagerhole aimed to study the prey-predator relationship with a view to formulating better conservation strategies. He, along with his wife Fiona Sunquist, wrote the book *Wild Cats of the World* (2002). A gist of an interview with him is given below.

Q. You have said that Nagerhole is the pyramid of tiger country, that it is an ideal tiger habitat. What makes it so?

Nagerhole brings together a combination of dense coverage which tigers need for stocking and also for hiding their kills. This mix of forest types supports a diverse assemblage of ungulates like the gaur and the sambar in such numbers that it almost staggers one's imagination. When you look at some of the other places and see how much food is available, then you go to Nagerhole and see that it clearly rivals some of the East African sanctuaries in terms of food availability for the predator. And here probably is the best place for tigers, considering the entire basic requirement.

Q. What was the finding of the studies you conducted on the tiger in the terrai country in Nepal?

As you know, we radio-collared tigers in Chitawan National park in Nepal. The study was on how tiger cubs disperse when they grow up and how they establish their own ranges. This information is crucial to answer many questions in our effort to conserve tigers. What would be the adequate supply of prey and what would be the adequate cover? What makes a tiger choose a particular area? Does male and female dispersal behaviour differ? We got some interesting answers through radio-telemetry. There is no other way to get these details. You must remember that the tiger moves in the night, under dense cover. So the traditional binocular and notebook method just cannot be used here.

Q. When did the radio-collar method appear as a research tool?

It emerged in the late fifties and early sixties. I got involved in it in 1965 and have been using it for more than 25 years. The improvement in electronics in terms of weight reduction has greatly improved the efficiency of the method.

Q. This conflict between the tiger on the one side and man and livestock on the other… How can this be addressed?

You have a real problem there. As sanctuaries get isolated, the interface between animals and humans gets sharper. You should have buffer zones to reduce the problem.

Q. What is the main thrust that wildlife studies are taking these days in other parts of the world?

The main thrust for many carnivore studies is to try and get an idea of the densities, lay out social structure, try and look at mortality rates, dispersal and habitat.

Q. Has there been any comparative study of the habitats?

There is one study on in the Soviet Far-east on the Siberian tiger.

Q. What is your overview of wildlife management scene in India?

Clearly, the focus now is on setting aside some specific areas for wildlife management and also on Project Tiger. This has worked, at least at the initial level. In the long term, it requires more active management in terms of forest modification, because all indication now is that the prey population is getting reduced. I think on the whole Project Tiger has been a success. But I think if some way can be found of connecting the small patches of forests, it would be a greater success. Census methods should also be improved to get an accurate idea of actually how many animals you have. The overall indication is that the trend is up.

Q. You have criticized the pug mark census as being unreliable. Then what is the best method for tiger census?

Trying to conduct a census of any of the large carnivores, be it a tiger or a lion, is a difficult proposition indeed. There are certain facts you can get from the pug-mark method, like the male-female occurrence or the movement of any particular tiger. But to be effective, this method must be combined with some other. What I would like to see is some system which employs the line of transaction method to assess how much prey is available. We know roughly how much tigers eat. We should get an idea of the prey biomass, then we can say that this will support so many tigers. You can then compare this with the estimate you get out of the pug mark census. You can also set up camera traps. As I have pointed out, it should be a combination of methods.

Q. What do you think are the main threats to tiger in India?

As human population increases, you could have a small number of tigers in isolated pockets. These populations may carry on well for fifty years without any problem. Then with the isolation, you could end up with a population like zoo animals. They could have been cut off from the other population, would have been inbred and we know from captive breeding that inbreeding can be a serious problem.

Q. Do you think we have a viable population in the various sanctuaries in India that could avoid inbreeding?

In some places they are safe, like here in Nagerhole, Bandipur and Wynand areas, which are large. But in some cases, I think the stretch of forest is too small.

Q. How is your study with Ulhas Karanth in Nagerhole progressing?

Ulhas was my student at the University of Florida which has a huge international programme. When I met him in Mumbai at a meeting a few years back, I recognized that here was a man who could better the research we did on tigers in Chitawan in Nepal. I am saddened by the blocks put up to thwart his unbiased research.I hope he will be able to resume his work there soon.

(In 1993, The Forest Department in Karnataka revoked the permission given to Dr. Karanth to radio-collar tigers. This started a long debate on wildlife studies and radio-telemetry).

–

The Hindu

(15.08.1993)

Wildlife Studies And Conservation

An interview with Wildlife biologist Ulhas Karanth on his being awarded the Paul Getty Award for Conservation Leadership in 2006.

Q. Wildlife studies are increasing. More and more institutions for wildlife studies are coming up. And there is less and less wildlife left. How do you see this paradox?

I see this paradox in two ways. First, before we ask why there is less, we have to ask how there can be more. To deal with issues like human-wildlife conflict and competition for resources between wildlife and humans, you need a huge input of knowledge. It is not just a question of guarding it with a stick. Given the biodiversity and richness of wildlife in India, what we know is very little, in fact. What we know is nowhere on the scale it is required. Just imagine, 25% of the world's carnivores are in India, and we have maybe 50 practicing field biologists, which is pathetically low. So I see the paradox as being less knowledge rather than more. Even though we have young biologists coming up in this field, they find it difficult to work because of the tremendous constraints under which one has to work in India because of institutional structure mindset.

Q. That leads to my second question. The attitude of the Government, that is forest officials, towards field biologists has always been problematic. Why is this?

This is a major problem. I think the reasons are twofold. First, forest department is a law enforcement agency. Their primary aim is to keep their turf protected. It is a hierarchical system that does not tolerate any questioning. That is a mindset. Such a mindset is required for law enforcement. But it is not conducive to enquiry. Secondly, the need for wildlife studies and the need for its application can be appreciated only if there is an understanding of wildlife. Unfortunately, we do not have a cadre of professionally trained people taking care of wildlife. When I say professionally, I have in mind the kind of training a doctor or engineer receives.

In other domains such as agriculture, there was a sea change in the fifties. A professionalized cadre appeared on the scene. We have provision for professional training in agricultural universities. Whereas in wildlife, we do not want science. This has to be broken. The Prime Minister's Science Advisory Council should take note of this situation. The Ministry of Environment does not see this. Earlier generations of foresters such as Deb Roy and P. K. Sen (former Directors of Project Tiger) encouraged wildlife research. They gave permission for radio collaring tigers. They did not practice dog-in-the-manger policy. One would expect attitudes to be more liberal when a new generation takes over. That does not happen, by and large. There are certain individuals in the forest department who are pro-research and are helpful. But on the whole, it is a sad situation. Similarly, conservation NGOs, do not get any encouragement or assistance from the Establishment.

I think in the seventies, NGOs and Government had reasonably good synergistics. Many laws were launched at the instance of NGOs. In launching Wildlife Preservation Act and Forest Conservation Act, the NGOs played an important part. Whereas in the last five or ten years, the Ministry of Environment has taken systematic steps to dilute the conservation laws. In some cases, the Supreme Court had to intervene to stop this process. The wildlife establishment in our country has shifted away from its core mission of conservation. It has started supporting Industrial interests and corporate forces and their entry into the forest. This is the reason why NGOs and wildlife establishment have drifted apart. So you find a genuine conservationist or a passionate wildlifer being kept at arm's length. The official advisory bodies are filled with individuals who would listen to the establishment and with little knowledge of wildlife.

Q. That brings me to a related question. Very few wildlife biologists raise their voice when the government takes a step that is patently harmful to wildlife. Why don't they take a stand?

You have to see a dichotomy here. Conservationists like Valmiki Thaper, Belinda Wright, Chinnappa or Wildlife First have always stood up and fought for conservation. But wildlife scientists do not speak. One reason is the traditional hesitancy of a scientist. Even when they feel strongly about an issue and express themselves against it in private conservation, scientists do not take it to any public forum. If I alienate the government or someone powerful, what will be the consequence for my research, my funding and my academic advancement? I think often they are too cautious.

The second reason which is a real threat to academic freedom is that a lot of these biologists are working in institutions heavily funded by the government. Only as long as they have this cozy relationship, many wildlife scientists are assured of funding. When your survival is linked so strongly with government funding, you are hesitant. The way around this is that no institution should be guaranteed government funding. For funding it should compete on merit, complete with peer reviewing.

Q. In India, conservation has not become a people's movement. What, in your opinion, are the reasons?

I agree with this. For any movement to be widespread, the regional cultures and local language of the area have to play an important part. Conservation in India began more as a preoccupation of the more affluent section of society, largely the English-speaking section. It has remained confined to that. It is beginning to change but not fast enough. In outfits like Wildlife First and some other NGOs in Karnataka, their core people are from small towns. The movement has to percolate to small towns like Chikmagalur and Tirunelveli. It has to enter the typical Indian middle-class household.

But this has not happened, and one reason is that there is no material in local languages for people to read. They read something from the Sunday supplements of dailies. That seems to be the only source if they want to read anything about wildlife in local languages. Regional language television plays no role in conservation.

Q. One last question. How do you see the future of the tiger in India? A lot has happened since you wrote *The Way of The Tiger* in which you had expressed optimism.

Jim Corbett had predicted in the thirties that the tiger will be extinct by 1950. People have been making such doomsday prophesies for a long time. In the nineties, they said it will be 2000, now they say by 2020 the tiger will be gone. I really do not believe in such predictions because it involved two factors: one is how technology and society change. Second is how we respond to a given situation. It depends upon what we do now. If we say we do nothing, the number of tigers will go down. Where people are doing the right things on the ground, tigers will survive. But how many such places will be there will depend on what we do now. I know that there will be wild tiger population. But how many such places will be there across India, that is the big question.

–

The Hindu

(14.10.2007)

The Lost Orchid Of Agasthyamalai

When I received an invitation in 2011 for dinner by botanical historian Henry Noltie of the Royal Botanical Garden Edinburgh, I was thrilled. I had heard about his research, particularly the three-volume work on Robert Wight, who in 1836, trekked around Palani ranges and documented the botanical wealth of the area. In the years that followed, there has been renewed curiosity in early botanists of British India and Noltie's work on the subject is considered seminal. My own interest in meeting him was to learn about the British botanist Drury. Over dinner, Henry talked about Drury.

Heber Drury (1819-72) was a Colonel in the Madras Light Infantry stationed in Travancore, He wrote the *Handbook of the Indian Flora* (3 vol) and the *Useful Plants of India.* Incidentally, the *Handbook* is dedicated to the Prince of Travancore, showing that Drury was not the usual snobbish Raj Officer of that era. The British government was interested in knowing the commercial potential of the plants in their tropical colonies, while naturalists like Drury were interested in the plants as subjects of study. As an adjunct to this study, a school of botanical painting developed in South India. We have a volume of drawings of grasses made by a 'native' artist whom Drury employed while in Travancore.

His autobiography *Reminiscences of Life & Sport in Southern India* (London: W. H. Allen & Co., 1890) provides a window in the natural history of the period.

Drury's other claim to fame is that a rare orchid of the Western Ghats has been christened after him. *Paphiopedilum drury* is endemic to the Agasthya ranges near Tirunelveli, better known as the Courtallam ranges, almost at the southern end of the Western Ghats. This area has now been recognized as one of the hot spots of biodiversity in the world. Incredibly rich in life forms, these hills are traditionally known for herbs and medicinal plants. The orchid we are talking about , *Paphilopedilum drury* grows on the grassy slopes of these ranges and blooms in May-June, a yellow coloured flower of 5-7 cm diameter. There was another G. D. Drury, Collector of Tirunelveli, whom I had earlier mistaken to be the orchid Drury.

Known among orchid fanciers as "the Lost Orchid", *P. drury* is now a much sought-after collector's item. I have only seen a pressed specimen in the herbarium of the Botanical Survey of India, Coimbatore. There was an orchid fancier in Bengaluru who had two plants, but would not trust me enough to let me photograph them. What is special about this plant is that it is one of the relict species; that is, this species is found in the Himalayas and next only in the Western Ghats, but nowhere in between. The red Rhododendron is another relict plant. Among mammals we have the tahr – the Nilgiri tahr here and the Himalayan tahr there – as relict specie; among birds the Grey-headed flycatcher is a relict species.

The lost orchid came to symbolize the disappearing floral wealth and the amazing biodiversity of the Western Ghats. To raise money to save such rare botanical species of the world, plant artist Stone chose to paint the Lost Orchid and sold it to raise money.

When I first learnt about this orchid in the early 1970s, I was naïve enough to think that all you have to do is to walk around in this area and you will see the plant. I went searching for it in Courtallam. That was a memorable trek, but I did not see the orchid. It was only later that I learnt that this is a plant of grasslands and that this terrestrial orchid is noticeable only during the flowering season. It belongs to a variety popularly referred to as "Lady's slipper orchid" after the shoe-shaped flower Paphilopedilum. There are quite a few of this variety in the Himalayas and the North-East but only one in Western Ghats.

It was only 42 years later that I was able to set my eyes on this iconic orchid. On learning that an orchid collector in Bangalore has this plant I called him. After close questioning he gave me this address. I had to promise that I will share neither his address nor his phone number with any one else. In his home, one whole floor is devoted to orchids. There is periodical, automatic spraying and also classical music. He believes that plants respond to music. He has two plants of the orchid I was looking for and they were in bloom. I was permitted to photograph it. (photo pg.138)

Quite a number of the books on Natural History written during the Raj era are getting resurrected, some through reprint and some through an electronic form in the Net. This is providing us with new insights about the pioneers, their work and the incredible wealth of wildlife in those years.

–

The Hindu
(07.09.2008)

The Book And The Man

If one were to point out a single individual who has contributed most to the conservation movement in India, it would be Salim Ali. His *Book of Indian Birds*, first published in 1942, changed the way many people looked at the world around them. It won countless converts to bird watching Once you take to birding, your concern widens into basic environmental issues. This is a logical journey numerous people have taken in India. Many biologists who contributed significantly to wildlife protection began as bird watchers. Salim Ali wrote prolifically on birds and on conservation, even as his field guide kept being republished with unfailing regularity.

He believed that bird behaviour should be documented so that other researchers can follow up. This meant observing birds in their habitats. So he undertook a series of surveys in different parts of India; in this effort, he was assisted by some princely states. It was out of the notes taken during these surveys that the *Book of Indian Birds* grew. At a time when most bird studies were done in laboratories, with emphasis on taxonomy, Salim Ali was in the field peering through his binoculars and taking notes. One day, he was riding a camel in the Rann of Kutch to see the flamingo city and on another, trekking in Ladakh to locate the breeding grounds of the Black-necked crane. As a result of Salim Ali's example, wildlife life studies gained more field orientation in India. All his reports and notes were published.

Now, Tara Gandhi, his former student, has collected his varied works, meticulously edited them, organized them and has produced this impressive two volume work. The writings span from 1907, when young Salim Ali as a school student wrote his first note on a bird, to 1987, the year he died. It includes his writings, speeches, extracts from books, questions asked by him in Parliament and interviews. It is a rich selection from the works of one who played a key role in getting the conservation movement going in India, truly a fitting tribute by a student to her teacher.

The editor has organized the papers according to topics, such as Bird Behaviour, Bird Surveys, History of Indian Ornithology, and so on. A crisp introduction to each section provides the background. The writings in each section are organized chronologically, which enables readers to see the evolution of certain concepts. There are quite a few extracts from Salim Ali's autobiography *The Fall of a Sparrow*. Interestingly, there is a book of the same title, from the realm of Christian Theology, a reference to Jesus talking about how God takes care of even a lowly sparrow.

Not just Indian birds, there are also stories about exotics. For instance, there is a moghul miniature, now in the Hermitage museum in Leningrad, which depicts a dodo. There are only two illustrations done from a live specimen of the bird and this is one of them. It was on the basis of these drawings that a museum exhibit of a dodo was recreated. It is displayed at the Natural History museum of New York. Salim Ali traces the fascinating history of this miniature painting in his paper titled 'Bird Study in India: Its history and Importance'.

Many legends of Indian ornithology come alive in these pages. The story of the discovery of the flamingo city in the Rann of

Kutch, the re-discovery of the Jerdon's Courser, Salim Ali's trek to Manasarovar and the agitation to save the Silent Valley. There are profiles of naturalists who worked with Salim Ali, including Loke Wan Tho, the bird photographer and Ralph Morris, the planter of Biligiriranga hills. I searched for any reference to the notorious Richard Meinertzhagen, who was associated with Salim Ali on some trips and left nasty references about the old man. But did not find any.

The anthology is not just about birds. It's about issues, concepts and history. In the section on Moghul emperors, Salim Ali writes about mammals that figure in their notes. So you read 16th century records of Abul Fazl and Jahangir about the wild ass, the Black buck and the Gangetic dolphin. The emperor seemed to have had a special regard for Sarus crane and wrote lengthy notes about this bird. He was particularly impressed with their monogamous pairing and mentions observing a pair with two young ones in Gujarat.

Salim Ali, with great foresight, saw the danger to the conservation movement from animal rights groups. He wrote in his *Fall of the Sparrow*: "I consider the current trend of conservation education given to the young on grounds of ahimsa alone – something akin to preservation of holy cows – unfortunate and totally misplaced." We see the result of such teaching now. The conservation movement is in danger of being hijacked by animal rights, and with disastrous results. While putting down his view on shikar in 1976, Salim Ali makes a mention of the destruction caused by armed forces. He added that though the army had stopped shooting wildlife, the para military forces kept on killing. He truthfully recorded himself shooting thousands of birds for scientific purposes. It was before wildlife photography and high-resolution binoculars. And there were plenty of birds around.

One of the strong points of Salim Ali was his ability to articulate in writing. Not many scientists are gifted with this talent. One can see his writing skill getting honed over the years. They have the minimalist character of a Japanese painting. Sample this: "A bird has been accurately defined as a feathered biped. Although in the popular mind flight is the most characteristic attribute of a bird, there are some birds that do not fly (e.g. the Ostrich) whereas there are some other animals besides birds that do (e.g. bats and insects). Feathers, therefore, are the chief characteristic of birds: no other animal has them and no bird is without them."

These writings encompass not just the history of bird study in India, but the milestones in the conservation movement. For instance, he was instrumental in persuading the Government to set up a Department of Environment, thus gaining some control over projects. Like M. Krishnan, Salim Ali also held the view that forest and wildlife should have been in the hands of Central Government. While participating in the Silent Valley movement, he recorded, "Projects of far reaching importance are begun without giving sufficient prior publicity to the proposed or adequate opportunity for public debate upon its possible consequences. The decisions are often based largely on short-term regional economic benefits and take little count of the inherent ecological hazards." It is so true, whether it is Sethusamudram project in Tamil Nadu or the 6- lane road to Salem.

Hyderabad-based archivist Ashish Pittie monitored writings on birds in India and prepared a massive electronic database *A Bibliographic Index to the Ornithology of Indian Region* (1995). He prepared this basically from the *Journal of BNHS* and also included other sources such as *The Newsletter for Birdwatchers*. This has come in handy for the editor of these two volumes. The world of twitchers has been transformed with the arrival of cyberspace communication. One such is the database that Pittie has painstakingly prepared.

These two volumes have been designed and produced with great care, complete with reader-friendly fonts. However, I missed two features in this work. One is an index. An index tremendously increases the value and utility of a book of this nature, particularly when it is an anthology. I think it is as important as the contents page. In the age of word processors, it is easy to get it done. There is not even an index of the birds mentioned in the book. Secondly, and this is not so indispensable, is a list of Salim Ali's works that are in public domain but not included in this collection. This would have been of help to researchers.

–

A Bird's Eye View: The Collected Essays and Shorter Writings of Salim Ali. Edited by Tara Gandhi. Two volumes. Hard cover. Rs. 1495. Permanent black. 2006 New Delhi

The Hindu
(24.04.2010)

The Man Who Painted The Lilies

"O. T. Ravindran might do for the weeds and wild flowers of India what James Audubon did for the birds of America," wrote a reviewer after seeing an exhibition of his paintings at the Carnegie Art Center in Washington in 1984.

OT, for his friends – O for Orchids and T for trees, he would say – had many labels: horticulturist, landscape designer, ecologist, botanist and painter. However, it was as an accomplished plant artist that he was known the world over. When his four paintings of orchids were brought out as stamps in 1991, the series was hailed by philatelists; for quite a few years, special albums of these stamps was gift items in our embassies abroad. The Smithsonian museum in Washington has his paintings as exhibits and Kew Gardens in London has them in its holdings.

Fascinated by plants and trees that surrounded him in his village in Kerala, Ravindran started drawing even as a schoolboy. This interest led him to graduate in Botany in Madras Christian College, where he came under the influence of his professor, the legendary Dr. Venkatasubban. A self-taught artist, Ravindran kept up his painting.

Unconventional in many ways, he discouraged visitors. preferring to be alone. "Lot of people call me a nut case," he once wrote, "since I spend most of my time with plants, especially wild ones." Whenever I wanted to see him, I would go unannounced and take my chance. I got to know OT in the seventies when we served in the WWF committee. His knowledge of plants and trees was phenomenal, and he was willing to share it. His dedication to his calling was amazing. He always painted from a *in situ* live specimen. If he learnt that an orchid was blooming in Yercaud, he would pack his painting kit and be at the railway station in a few hours. He would visit the plant in various seasons and capture its different appearances in one canvas, something you cannot do in a photograph. He set exacting standards for himself. His aim was to be morphologically accurate and at the same time create something elegant to look at. It was a fine balance that he always achieved. Western Ghats was his favourite haunt. He observed that over the years, the floral wealth was dwindling and many plants, such as the fabled Kurinji, were getting rare. OT had sent an outstanding drawing of Kurinji flower to be used in a postage stamp and was campaigning for it. When the stamp eventually did come out, it carried a mugshot of a bunch of Kurinji, not his painting. This saddened him immensely.

Plant artists are rare in India. During the British period, particularly after the founding of the School of Arts and Crafts in Chennai, a few Indian artists were commissioned to paint plants for the sake of scientific record. Other than this, there was no tradition of botanical art. This may be one reason why OT got noticed more in the West than in India. His work went largely unrecognized here. "My friends in India, worldly as they are, may now have more reason to call me the craziest artist they know. But I revel in satisfaction that more unusual people have gone before me such as Thoreau and Johnny Appleseed. The philosophy or nature of those peculiar men may raise criticism, but if properly understood, it would make the world a much more clean and beautiful place for all of us to live in."

Though he did not write much, he was a fine writer, as readers of his occasional columns in *The Hindu* know. Here is a sample of his style from a piece he wrote about a cactus. "Plants, especially natural ones (as opposed to those artificially made) have a vibrancy of their own. They only need our help to bring out the beauty in them. Even the weed growing unnoticed in the thicket is strikingly beautiful. Plant them, sketch them and arrange them and they become pieces of fine art. Art, whatever man may claim it to be, is nothing but his sincere effort to imitate the unattainable perfection that is Nature."

–

The Hindu
(24.12.2006)

COUNTING THE NILGIRI TAHR

E. R. C. Davidar (Reggie for his friends) who passed away on 7th April 2007 in Puducherry at 87 was one of the early advocates of wilderness and its creatures at a time when there were very few who spoke up for them. He operated in an era when the work of environmental protection had not been institutionalized.

As secretary of the Planters' Association in the Nilgiris, Davidar (one of his ancestors was David Nadar) got interested in wildlife through hunting. Based in Ooty and Coonoor since 1952, he came to know the Nilgiris like the palm of his hand. As the Honorary Superintendent of The Nilgiris Game Association, he took a series of pioneering steps for conservation in this wildlife rich area. He enlisted the cooperation of the licensed hunters – before the Wildlife Protection Act of 1972 had banned hunting – for conservation of wildlife in the Nilgiris. In 1963, with the help of shikaris in the Nilgiris, he studied the status of Nilgiris tahr, the elusive mountain goat endemic to Western Ghats.

After the passage of the Wildlife Protection Act, he made the Nilgiri Game Association undergo a metamorphosis. He created awareness about conservation in this area. In 1975, he conducted a detailed census of the tahr; through the *Journal of the Bombay Natural History Association*, he announced that his observations that there were only 2200 tahr left. On the basis of this finding, the animal entered the *Red Data Book of the International Union for Conservation of Nature* and plans were drawn for its conservation. On reading his notes on tahr, wildlife biologist George Schaller came to the Nilgiris looking for him and stayed with him in Coonoor. In his book *The Stones of Silence*, Schaller paid glowing tributes to Davidar's work on conservation of tahr; Davidar, in turn, learnt the techniques of field work from Schaller.

Davidar was an archetypical "huntin' shootin' fishing" planter. He once told me the story of how he got a cattle-lifting leopard near Devarshola by squatting inside the pen with his rifle on the ready. He bagged the leopard at close range when it came for its weekly fix of sheep. His contemporary conservationist and friend M. Krishnan used to mock at his combination of hunting and conservation. "Reggie wants to preserve wildlife on the walls of his drawing room," he would say. A keen angler, Davidar knew all the spots in this part of the country where you could land trout or masheer. He had recorded the abundance of masheer in Amaravathi River near Udumalaippettai. After the dam was built in the fifties, the masheer disappeared.

Davidar retired in 1981 and devoted his time to conservation. He continued his work on Nilgiri tahr and drew the attention of biologists to the precarious situation of this mountain goat. This was a time before gadgets like cell phones and GPS equipment had come into use. Davidar trekked the habitats of the tahr, the mountain fastness of Munnar and Palani ranges of the Western Ghats, often holing up in caves for the night and produced a seminal report. His daughter Priya accompanied him on many treks. (One of the early students of Salim Ali, she is now the Dean of Life Sciences in Pondicherry University.) The articles he published in the *Journal of the Bombay Natural History Society* and *Sanctuary* magazine are evidences of his commitment to field work. It was a purely voluntary job for him at a time when there were very few wildlife biologists doing field work.

Active in this field for nearly forty years, he survived an attack by a Gaur that was surprised by his approach in the forest. 'It did all that a Gaur could do," he later wrote to me in an inland letter. 'It threw me in the air, gored me and trampled me." Davidar came out of the hospital in one piece and lived the rest of his life in his rural lair at Padappai, near Vandalur, continuing to plough his lonely furrow. The last time I met him in Padappai, he was in fact supervising ploughing in his field. Padappai, incidentally, is a housing colony of the Davidar clan and was inaugurated by Lord Atlee sometime in the mid-forties. A small sign board at the entrance to colony announces this historic incident.

Davidar's book *The Chital Walk: Living in the Wilderness* (OUP,1997) is a collection of delightful essays on his experiences in the forest around his eponymous property on the periphery of Mudumalai sanctuary. He lived in this place for some months every year and collected much local lore. One such was the story of bandit Veerappan, locally known as Mozhukkan. Davidar put down what he learnt about the legendary brigand in *Jungle Tales*. The book did not get the notice it deserves due to the unfortunate title. Actually the title Davidar had given was *The Night of the Tusker.*

One of the lesser known dimensions of Davidar's work is his writings for children. Published by National Book Trust, titles such as *Adventures of a Wildlife Warden* combine natural history and a gripping narrative. The other title is *Fables from the Jungle*, in which he writes about the behaviour of 14 creatures under chapters such as "Why the Hyena laughs". His story *Hunting the Cross Tusker*, about tranquilizing and treating a wounded elephant, published in the International edition of *Readers' Digest*, gained wide attention. When he visited U S for the first time, he recorded his experiences in a memorable article, sprinkled with puckish humour, in *Span*. In all his writings, his deep involvement with the external world comes through.

He had a captivating style of writing. Sample this. Writing about a stream in front of his property in Masinagudy, he records, "Jungle streams are very communicative. The stonier the bed, the chattier they are. Sigurhalla had a lusty musical voice when we first made its acquaintance. It was a delight to listen to. Its song was never repetitive. There was a new tune with every change in the water-level and the tone varied as the composition of the bed varied. One had only to tune in his imagination to read the music."

–

The Hindu
(24.10.2010)

Bird Calls In Your Drawing Room

One of the memorable experiences in my years of bird watching has been listening to the song of Shama, listed among the world's most famous song-birds, in 1994 in Kandala Bird sanctuary, near Mumbai. Standing transfixed behind a rock that misty morning and listening, I wondered if anyone could record this ethereal sound of the forest.

Young Sivaprasad of Coimbatore had done just that. A computer engineer by profession, he spent years watching the birds of Western Ghats. In the recent past, he roamed the wilderness around Coimbatore and Wyanad with a microphone and recorded the calls of 66 birds, ranging from the Crested Hawk eagle to the Mottled Wood owl. His cassette "An Audio Guide to the Birds of South India", released in London, attracted a lot of notice. This cassette, a landmark in bird studies in India, is the first work of its kind in the sub-continent and Sivaprasad achieved this almost single-handedly. This cassette is the first of the series he plans to bring out.

Recording the calls of birds is new to Indian ornithology. The only information on bird calls available to us is in the bird books which give the nearest sounding English words. Calls of certain birds struck the early birdwatchers, British all, as very similar to some English words: they described these calls with those words: for instance the call of a Yellow-wattled lapwing as 'Did-he-do-it' or the call of the Common-hawk cuckoo as 'Brain-fever… Brain-fever'. Such descriptions do not give any idea of the call. Moreover, some species which look very much alike but with diverse calls – kingfishers for instance – can easily be identified by their distinct calls. In dealing with nocturnal birds like owls and nightjars, calls are critical. The call of a bird is a surer guide to its identification than its colouration or flight. But then one has to be well acquainted with bird calls.

That is where Sivaprasad comes in. His audio guide introduces the calls of different birds. An announcement, of the popular and scientific name of the bird, done impeccably by Krys Kasmierszak, precedes each recording. Then comes the call. A booklet, giving the names of the birds, the number assigned to it in Salim Ali & Ripley's 'Handbook', the location and the time of recording, in addition to explaining the background sounds if any, comes with the tape. Such recording facilitates closer and detailed analysis of bird calls and their various uses. This new science is called Ontogeny. The recorded tapes can be fed into a spectrograph, which transforms the sound into visual signs for comparative study.

Birds call for many reasons: to keep in touch with the others of the group, to announce the availability of food, on sensing danger or while in distress. The 'aung…aung' of the migrating Bar-headed goose is to keep in touch with co-travelers. The Koel's popular song is a call for mating. An ornithologist observed that a starling's heart-beat was faster when it heard the distress call of another starling. Among the nocturnal birds like the owl and the night heron, calls are much more consequential. They rely entirely on sound to locate mates and rivals. Understandably their calls are distinct and carry far. Birds in dense vegetation, where visibility is limited, also have loud and distinct calls.

A bird's song has been described as an audible fence. Usually associated with breeding, a song is different from a call. The bird announces that the territory has been occupied and that it will be defended. A song can often be an invitation to mate and breed. The Magpie robin's song which can be heard often even in our urban gardens is part of its effort to impress the female. While birds of the open country, like peacocks and sarus cranes indulge in elaborate dances to woo the mate, birds of the forest sing.

To record bird calls, in addition to equipment like directional microphone and parabolic reflector, you need enormous patience. First of all, you should be knowledgeable on bird behaviour and should know where to go for which species. One should also anticipate calls.

Sivaprasad says he waited for a whole day to record a single call. The recordist should be alert and should have a steady hand or else handling noises will also be recorded. The right season should be chosen to work. For example in summer you cannot find a single spot in the forests of South India where you do not have cicadas or bush crickets keeping up their chorus. The forest floor will also be covered with dried leaves which will make crackling noise when you move.

The quality of recording in this 90-minute tape is of high order. Sivaprasad has managed to capture on tape the calls of rare species like Malabar trogon, a colourful bird that inhabits the interior of rain forests. It is difficult even to spot it. The calls of birds like the Heart-spotted woodpecker evokes the ambience of the forests of Western Ghats effectively.

Dim the lights put on this tape in your music system and let the trilling song of the Malabar whistling thrush fill your drawing room. A truly transcendental experience.

–

The Hindu
(12.02.1982)

Romulus Whitaker

Divya Mudappa and Shankar Raman

Ian Lockwood

Paradise Flycatcher

Rhododendron tree

Tiger relaxing on the river Bank in Badra sanctuary

Dog and friends

OT Ravindran

Lady's slipper orchid by OTR

ERC Davidar

Nilgiri tahr with kid

Magpie-Robin

Issues

The Seasons Of Life

American poet Maya Angelou's mother had a visitor one day who went on complaining about the weather. After she left, the old lady turned to Maya and said, "There are people all over the world who went to sleep last night and did not wake again. Their beds have become their cooling boards; their blankets have become their winding sheets. They would give anything for just five minutes of what she was complaining about." I have this quote pinned on the soft board in my study, a constant reminder to be thankful for each day I wake up alive.

You meet people whose opening gambit for conversation is griping about the weather. "It is not so much the heat that bothers me," they explain. "It is the humidity." When the weather was cooler a few months ago, when the mornings were misty, the nip in the air heralded a cooler day and the koel called its heart out, I did not see them observing it or doing anything to celebrate the weather.

This season of summer that we grumble about has its many delights. It is the season for flowers in this part of our country. The Indian Laburnum tree, of which there are many in South Chennai, transforms into a golden canopy. Lots of other trees blossom in summer: the rain tree, the neem and the silk cotton. Some trees start sprouting new shoots in summer, like the Pungamia.

Different types of jasmine bloom and make your evenings magical A terrestrial orchid of Tamil Nadu, the Golden Vanda, puts out flowers in the sizzling heat of April.

Trees and plants that bloom and fruit in summer fill us not only with scent and taste, but also with memories. I am reminded of my college days when the Copperpod flanking the mud roads in the campus in Tambaram, would break into a riot of yellow and carpet the ground beneath in the early morning. That sight announced the approaching examinations and the holidays that would follow. Brought from Malaysia, it has been here long enough to acquire a Tamil name: *Perungkonrai.*

Even the Gulmohar tree, an exotic, celebrates the season by blossoming. The flowers attract a host of birds. The fluid, mellow calls of the Golden Oriole comes floating through rain trees, even as the early rays of sun hit its branches. Sunbirds visit these trees. Butterflies appear from nowhere and are all around you. When the sun warms up, the drumming calls of the Coppersmith float through the branches of avenue trees. I open the window of my study and see the Painted bat, roosting in the foliage of a monstera creeper, already asleep after a night's wandering, covering its body with its bright red and black wings.

Beginning with the celebrated *Chitra pournami*, moonlight takes on an ethereal quality in the hot months. It seems to be brighter and the sky clearer. The early morning and evening sunlight acquires a refulgent golden hue. And the sunsets turn dramatic. If you are in the countryside, watch the setting sun of summer. The sun appears larger as it sinks down the horizon like a gigantic sliver of fire. Each second, the colour pattern in the western horizon keeps changing dramatically. The sunset over Adyar estuary in Chennai is spectacular in summer.

In fact, the idea of clear-cut seasons is alien to us. We have borrowed, along with the English language, the four-fold classification of seasons of their part of the world, which has little relevance to the seasons here. This labelling does not fit with what we experience in India. Ours is a tropical land where there is no autumn or spring. Here, the transition from one season to the next here is almost imperceptible. Traditionally, till a hundred years ago, we had a six-fold classification of seasons: Here they are: Ilavenil (Chithirai-Vaikasi, April-May), Mudhuvenil (Ani-Aadi, June-July), Kaar (Aavani-Purattasi, August-September), Koodhir (Aippasi-Karthigai, October-November) Munpani (Markazhi-Thai, December-January) and lastly Pinpani (Masi-Panguni, February-March). This nomenclature describes our climate with a lot more meaning and acceptability.

And for me, the ultimate delight of summer is the mango. First tentatively and then in loads they start arriving. We just have to walk a few yards from our home and there they are: Banganapalli, Malgova, Dilpasand, Padhiri, Rumani, Senduraa and the humble Salem. Irresistible. I am convinced that the fruit Eve seduced Adam with was the mango and that the divine chroniclers slipped in documenting.

I think we have to accept summer, not because we cannot do otherwise, but because of the delights it holds. And that goes for the seasons of our lives too.

–

The Hindu
(01.05.2005)

School For Dogs

On a crisp December morning, a group of us dog enthusiasts assembled in a compound in Harrington Road in Chennai, with our pets on leash. Purpose? Orientation training for dogs would be shown for the first time in the ensuing dog show. Not just the dogs, but some of the owners like me, were also first timers as exhibitors in a show. We were instructed how to show our dog to the best advantage and what is looked for in each breed. Three volunteers from the Kennel Club of India were there to train. The dogs came in a variety of shapes and colours, from the low-slung Dachshunds to the stocky and formidable Rottweilers.

When there are different breeds of dogs, some bred for specific purposes, it is essential that their distinct features are retained and developed. For instance, in Denmark, Great Danes were used as guard dogs that trotted alongside horse drawn coaches. Though these are no longer used for the original task, dog shows ensure that breed characteristics are maintained. By being competitive, these shows set standards in dog care and breeding. They make dog fanciers realize that ownership of a dog carries with it responsibilities, not unlike that of parenthood. As Barbara Wodehouse, a Guru among dog-trainers, says, "There are no troublesome dogs. Only irresponsible owners."

Understandably, it was in Great Britain, the most dog-minded nation, that the first dog show was held, in Newcastle to be precise, in 1859. In the early shows, only Pointers and Setters, breeds that are described as "gun dogs" were admitted. The idea of dog shows quickly caught on and were held in the colonies also. The English Kennel Club, founded in 1879, set the pattern for all other kennel clubs that came up all over the world, including the club in Chennai, which was founded in 1896. Kennel clubs from 30 countries were affiliated to this mother club. Even now the standards and guidelines developed by the English Kennel Club for dog shows form the basis all over the world, including India. Most of the shows in India are held in winter and the well-known ones are in Mumbai, Delhi, Kolkata, Pune and Chennai. The show at Ooty, of course, is usually in May.

In Chennai that morning, Col. Gulrajani, the instructor, told the handlers that the idea of the exercise is to show the dog in such a way that its special features are emphasized. First your dog should get used to the proximity of other dogs so that it can be relaxed in the ring with all the other dogs around. And then you go on to the technique of actual showing. How to show small dogs like a Lhasa Apso and how to show big ones like a Doberman? The colonel told us that you walk fast when showing a small breed, and jog while with a large dog. This part of the training – walking the dog in the ring – is crucial. While you walk the dog in the ring, the judge watches its movements, the limb formations and its demeanour.

The second phase is you stack your dog for the judge to examine it closely; it should be still when the judge runs his hand over its body to feel its limbs and check the dentition. The dog should enjoy doing this work and should not appear as if it is suffering the handler. With the thoroughness characteristic of the army, the colonel instructed us what footwear to wear while showing a dog in the ring.

When I actually went to the show grounds with my dog, I was to learn more. You have to rest your dog between each event. You soon learn the jargon of show veterans, such as "Your fellow is sure to get a B.O.B." (Best of Breed). I noticed that the exhibitors' profile has changed. It is no more the preserve of the WOGs. Dog fanciers come from all walks of life. Ask the owners of stalls that sell doggy material in the show grounds. It is clear that there is one concern that unites all of them – the superintendents of the show, the judges, the ring stewards, the exhibitors, the volunteers of Veterinary College and the spectators – their love for dogs.

In recent decades, the Indian canine heritage has been receiving some welcome attention. In the shows these days you get to see Indian breeds like Rampur hound, Tibetan mastiff and Rajapalayam. In the 2005 year show in Chennai, there was a gem that did not receive the notice it deserved. Selvanayagam showed his Chippiparai perfect specimen, complete with a black muzzle. These dogs, along with the other breeds from Southern Tamil Nadu, like Rajapalayam and Kombai, were used for military purposes during the Poligar wars in the 19th century. The Poligar soldiers would creep close to the camp of the East India Company forces and unleash the dogs, who would charge to the stables, attack the hamstrings of the horses and immobilize them. Nelson records in *Madura Manuel* that often a horse would be exchanged for a Kombai dog.

By the time the show wound up, it was late in the evening. We collected our certificates and trophies and walked towards the gate, with our little fox terrier in tow. We felt we had grown to understand him and his world better.

–

The Hindu
(15.02.2001)

Who Speaks For The Jarawas?

If you drive along the road leading to Mayabandar from Port Blair in the Andamans, you might catch a glimpse of the Jarawas, one of the indigenous tribe of the islands. Often, they come out of their jungle homes to accept fruits and coconuts from visitors. With white teeth gleaming in the background of dark skin, the children look like so many ebony carvings. The story of the Jarawas has been the same as that of vanishing people elsewhere in the world, until a group of concerned people came forward to speak for them.

Saving Andaman and Nicobar Ecology (SANE), a non-governmental organization based in Port Blair, has taken up the cause of the Jarawas and sought legal remedies. On the 9th of April 2001, the Circuit bench of the High Court of Calcutta sitting in Port Blair passed a significant order. It directed the Central Government and the Andaman and Nicobar Administration to form a committee of experts, including sociologists, nutritionists and doctors to study the problems of the Jarawas.

Inhabitants of the dense rain forests of the Andaman Islands, the Jarawas have been living for millennia as hunter-gatherers, as an integral part of the ecosystem that harbours an incredible wealth of biodiversity. In the last century, loggers, poachers and settlers pillaged the forests, dooming the fate of the hapless Jarawas. Reduced to just 350 to 400, they are teetering on extinction. Hidden from civilization and resisting all attempts at contact, they had kept to themselves, never mixing with other people. In October 1997, in an inexplicable move, a group of Jarawas ventured out of their forest hideout and made contact with urban folks. And this has triggered a cascade of problems, provoking SANE to take up their cause.

Before intervening in a Public Interest Litigation petition in the High Court, SANE – led by one of its founders Samir Acharya, an islander – went about the task of collecting data on indigenous people. They contacted leading anthropologists and sociologists all around the world – many of whom were familiar with the issues connected with the indigenous people of A&N islands – and recorded their views. SANE studied the position of indigenous people elsewhere in the world, such as Brazil and Canada. Equipped with the formidable data, they moved the court.

Dr. Vishvajit Pandya, anthropologist of Victoria University, New Zealand, who had studied the indigenous people of Andamans, opined that the Jarawas should be made culturally safe and that policymakers should take a well thought out stand on the future of the Jarawas. Stephen Corry, of the Survival International, said that small populations of tribal people are unlikely to survive the effects of sedentarisation. He cautioned that settlement of the Jarawas in a reserve – a common but disastrous solution – would constitute a violation of their human rights. The lives of many indigenous peoples are linked to the specific topography of their land and relocation can wipe them off the face of Earth. Other experts warned that the Jarawas' contact with other people might cause serious medical problems to the tribe. Extinction through an epidemic is a reality, just a single infection away.

Indigenous people such as the Jarawas may hold the key to some mysteries of human history. Recent DNA studies point out that the Jarawas are closely related to the Bushmen of Africa. If proved, this will lend support to the Out of Africa theory of human descent. The proponents of this theory say that humans left Africa about 100,000 years ago and moved on land westward, eventually reaching Asia. Peter Bellwood, an anthropologist at the Australian National University, Canberra, suggests that these migrants came to Andamans about 35,000 years ago when the islands were connected by land to the Arakan mountain ranges of Myanmar. Later, when the sea rose, cutting off the land and creating many pockets of elevated land, people survived in these islands and developed distinct culture and language. In fact, their languages may contain keys to the riddle of human migration. Their intimate knowledge of plants, birds and other creatures of the tropical jungle can provide new breakthroughs in medical science.

Samir Acharya spoke with passionate concern for the Jarawas. He pointed out that the attitude of the mainlanders is not very different from that of British colonizers towards Indians. The dominant society's belief – that the Jarawas are backward and need improvement – is actually a racist notion based on ethnocentric viewpoint. Similar attitudes towards indigenous people have been observed in USA, Canada, Australia and New Zealand. SANE pleaded in its petition to ban all contact with the Jarawas, to evict all encroachers, camps and outposts from their area and to close the Andaman trunk road to all traffic.

The Hon'ble High court, in their epoch-making order, directed the A & N administration to prevent poaching and stop anything that encourages the Jarawas to beg by the highway. The order also prohibited any new construction in the Jarawa territory and not to make any extension of the Andaman trunk road as it would cut right into the forests, the home of the tribal people for millennia. However, the main thrust of the order was the direction that the committee of experts should submit their report within six months. The final judgement in the case would be given after that.

In its present order, the court directed the A&N administration "to teach the local people that the Jarawas are not inferior but different." In a nonegalitarian society like ours, such a realization would indeed be dream come true.

–

(For more on Jarawas read *Action Plan to Save the Jarawas*, by Subramanya Nayudu. Centre for Future Studies, Pondicherry University 1999)

The Hindu

(03.12.2001)

Splitting A Habitat: Wildlife On The Road

The judgment of the Karnataka High Court delivered on 27th June banning night traffic on NH 212 that cuts through Bandipur sanctuary brings to an end the controversy that has been raging on this issue. Since the road passes through two other adjacent sanctuaries, Mudumalai in Tamil Nadu and Wayanad in Kerala, the verdict in effect extends protection to these sanctuaries.

Road kills are quite common in roads passing through forests. Last February, we were driving along the road from Coonoor to Kothagiri early one morning. Where the road passes through a shola we found a fresh roadkill, a Brown civet cat, a rare nocturnal predator endemic to the Western Ghats. In a similar incident a few years ago, I had come across the carcass of a Malabar civet, now feared extinct, near Karwar on the highway that runs along the sea coast.

Roadkill is just one of the many problems that come up when a highway passes through a wildlife habitat. A road splits the habitat into two, forcing many of the inhabitants to cross the road during their peregrination in search of food, water or a mate, risking their lives, like the cat we saw that morning. Roads often run through migratory routes, exposing the itinerant herds to danger. Patches of forests that had remained inviolate for eons are opened to human depredation and their very nature is changed by these roads. Careless travellers on these roads start forest fires causing immense damage. Domestic cattle that move in these roads pass on contagious diseases to wildlife, which has no immunity to certain illnesses. A few years ago, a rinderpest epidemic wiped out thousands of Gaur in the Mudumalai-Bandipur stretch. Roads facilitate ruthless exploitation of the forests by big companies. Wildlife biologist Ullas Karanth says, "I see with sadness roads intruding deep into the forests as the arms of multinationals, like the limbs of an octopus." When a series of hydro-electric projects and dams were started in the Western Ghats after Independence, they spelt doom to many stretches of forest areas.

However, roads are necessary and many arteries like the highway from Guwahati to Jorhat that runs through Kaziranga National Park were laid long before we had any idea of wildlife conservation. In such a situation, what we can do is to control the traffic in these roads. In some sanctuaries, the road is closed for traffic after sundown. Or an alternate route can be provided. The traffic in the state highway 17D that cuts through Nagerhole National park will soon be diverted through an alternate route that skirts the park. This issue had gone up to the Supreme Court and the Central Empowered Committee constituted to go into the question suggested this solution. The new route is longer by only three kilometres.

Another step that could be taken is to ensure that new roads are not laid inside prime forests. The proposal for a road through Pushpagiri sanctuary in Karnataka has been referred to the Central Empowered committee. Some years back, there was a proposal to lay a road connecting Papanasam in Tamil Nadu with Trivandrum. It would have cut across pristine forest area of Kalakad-Mundanthurai Tiger Sanctuary. Fortunately the idea was dropped.

Now and then, we hear talk of a railway line through Sathyamangalam forests. We should bear in mind that railway lines passing through Gir sanctuary and Rajaji national park routinely take their toll of wildlife. Between Coimbatore and Palakkad, at least seven elephants have been killed in the past two years. Trains can be slowed down in these stretches and hooting can be resorted to warn animals. All this needs some serious interdepartmental coordination, a factor rare in our country.

Even animals seem to know the risk they face while crossing these roads. Recently, a group of wildlifers was motoring from Bandipur to Mudumalai one evening when one of them spotted a tiger in a lantana bush by the side of the road. They reversed the jeep and switched off the engine. The cat waited in the bush for a considerable time for the road to be clear of any traffic. Evidently it was monitoring vehicle movement through sound, hiding inside the bush. When it was totally quite, it broke cover and crossed the road. It was a tigress in an advanced stage of pregnancy. As the animal walked leisurely into the forest on the other side, they had time to take a few photos. (photo appears elsewhere in this book.)

Be it a road, a dam or dredging an isthmus to make a shortcut for ocean liners, every single act of tampering with Nature has an ecological price to be paid. A society should know this price before it takes any such step.

–

The Hindu
(06.09.2009)

Tourism vs. Wildlife

Prince Sadruddin Aga Khan, former United Nations diplomat and an environmentalist, once said that of all the "isms" of the 20th century, we might find that "tourism" is the worst. Alp Action, the outfit he formed to save the Alps from degradation, identified tourism as the major threat to the Alpine ecosystem. Manila Declaration on World Tourism, released after the World Tourism Conference in 1989, also pointed out the threatening relationship between tourism and environmental degradation. The danger posed by tourism to ecosystems is being demonstrated in many countries, including India.

A few months ago at Thekkady, I watched a boat with at least a hundred tourists move closer to a herd of elephants on the bank. Leaning on one side, the visitors shouted at the elephants to provoke them into action. Later, when the boat reached the jetty, all the men got out and squatted along the water's edge as if in a bizarre ritual, and urinated. In Vedanthangal sanctuary, one of the earliest to get legal protection, buses go right up to the lake bund, disturbing the nesting birds and shattering the serenity of the place. In Ranganthittu, a mixed heronry near Srirangapatna, boatloads of tourists are taken close to the nesting birds. In some sanctuaries, at the height of the season, there are so many private vehicles inside the sanctuary that you begin to wonder if you are in Anna Salai, Chennai or inside a wildlife habitat.

What is forgotten in all these situations is that sanctuaries exist for the animals, birds and plants; tourism can only be incidental, to be accommodated only as far as it does not pose any threat to the creatures there. We humans, in our arrogance, seem to consider all creatures existing solely for our benefit and pleasure. The primary purpose of setting up sanctuaries is to conserve all living forms in that area. Tourism in wildlife has to be of a very different character. Nature-based tourism or eco-tourism is relatively unknown in India. Eco-tourism respects nature and aims at minimum impact. A mere trip into the wilderness is not eco-tourism. Often such trips have deleterious effect on wildlife if one is not sensitive to nature. (If you want to know more, see *Eco-tourism: Potentials and Pitfalls* by Elizabeth Boo. WWF. USA.1990.)

In our country we do not make the crucial distinction between resorts, monuments, pilgrim centres, picnic spots and sanctuaries. Every place is a picnic spot with freedom to litter and be noisy. The emphasis is still on recreation-based, vehicular traffic-based tourism. Visitors are not instructed on how to conduct themselves inside a wildlife refuge – that they have to be totally silent, not wear bright coloured clothes, and not wear perfumes. We are impervious to the environmental and ecological implications of tourism. Nature-based tourism is relatively unknown in India.

Tourists want to be shown something during their visit to a sanctuary. Till a few years ago, there used to be a "lion show" for tourists in Gir sanctuary in Gujarat. A domestic buffalo would be tied to a tree, lions would come, kill and eat it. Tourists who paid for the show could watch the lions feed. Wildlife researchers pointed out the damaging effect of this practice on the lions' behaviour and fortunately, the practice was stopped.

The danger inherent in wildlife tourism is that it could destroy the very phenomenon on which it depends, namely wildlife.

The fragility of the ecosystem could collapse with the impact of thousands of tourists, who in any case do not respect wildlife.

Tourism requires vehicular traffic inside sanctuaries; for this you need roads. What is the impact of a road in a forest? It splits the wilderness into two, creates a barrier for the movement of animals and fragments the habitat. It provides a conduit for exotic vegetation. In many of our sanctuaries, you can see parthenium all along the roadside. When you lay a road in a forest, you expose the soil to wind, rain and sun. So it dries up the land, which increases the chances of fire, both natural and through humans. Roads make the forests accessible not only to tourists but also to the timber mafia, poachers and film crews.

Just as the number of animals that can be sustained by a given patch of forest is limited, so is the number of tourists who can visit a sanctuary. It has to be determined how many tourists can be inside a sanctuary at any given time, without damaging it. And the comforts provided should be minimal. The higher the comfort level, the heavier will be the impact, in terms of pollution and staff required. There is one more problem in India. Professionally run nature tourism packages call for inter-departmental cooperation. Departments like forest, tourism, transport and fisheries have to coordinate, which is still a distant dream in India.

Advocates of tourism in sanctuaries point out the situation in African countries, where wildlife tourism has emerged as a major industry. After visiting a few sanctuaries in Africa, including the fabled Masai Mara, I realized there could be no comparison. The African Savannah and dry scrub jungle support a vast number of each species. In some spots, you see herds of animals up to the horizon. But in India, the absolute number of each species is dangerously low. There are may be six hundred lions, seven hundred rhinos, forty Sangai deer and so on. Also here in India we deal with fragile ecosystems, like rain forests and mangrove swamps. Add to this the fact that some of our national parks are just a few square kilometres, like Guindy National Park or Borivali National Park.

But most important, African wildlife refuges are run on professional lines, with unrelaxing standards. No private vehicles or thoroughfares inside a protected area. The cottages are of low height, much below the tree canopies and only colours merging with the forests are used. All signboards are on bare wood, with the letters burnt in. The guides are knowledgeable. In Masai Mara, the youngster who brought tea saw me watching birds outside my tent. Pouring the tea, he asked me if I had spotted the Tsavo purple-banded sunbird yet and went on to describe it in the lingo of a seasoned birder.

Such professionalism is absent in Indian sanctuaries, though there are a few exceptions. One such place is Kabini Lodge at the fringe of Nagerhole National Park in Karnataka. It is wildlife tourism run on professional lines. Knowledgeable guides, light impact on the ecosystem, and sound management. I am not familiar with the Nature Resort at Vythiri in the Wynad hills of Kerala, which I hear is also quite good in this respect.

Its impact will be light if the visitor is aware that the sanctuary exists basically for the flora and fauna and that spotting any animals is a matter of chance. Those who take eco-tourism seriously and go trekking, back-packing, bird watching, camping or river-running actually heighten their awareness of environment and will find the experience life enhancing.

–

The Hindu
(24.09.2000)

The Water Festival: Slipping From Memory

Recently I found myself at a meeting of some concerned citizens of the area we live in. The agenda was to discuss how we could observe the festival of *Aadi 18* and use the occasion to create an awareness of water conservation. I could hardly participate in the meeting as my mind kept going back to my childhood in my village on the banks of the Amaravathi.

In the Tamil month of *Aadi* (July-August) the rivers swell with water and people welcome it by celebrating the water festival *Aadi pathinettu.* On the morning of the eighteenth day of the month, the whole village congregates on the banks of the river, bearing mud plates of sprouted green grams, paddy and maize, a colourful procession moving towards the river at dawn. These plates would be dropped in the flood. Community cooking on the bank culminated in a feast of different varieties of rice: lime rice, tamarind rice, coconut rice and curd rice. I still recall the euphoria of sitting under a marudam tree on a wet muddy floor before a banana leaf covered with ghee rice. The boys would indulge in daring water sports like jumping into the torrent from overhanging tree branches or playing catch-as-can in the swirling waters. Even in the early seventies, I have watched the festival on the banks of the Kaveri in Trichy. It was a scene of great festivities. While the devotees thronged the Amman mandapam, youngsters would get into the passenger train in Trichy town station and jump into the turgid water as the train passed over the bridge across Kaveri. It was a celebration of nature, of life.

This festival is not related to the position of any celestial body, nor does it have any Puranic origin. Water festival is a common feature in quite a few Asian countries like Myanmar; the best known is the one observed in Thailand. Scholars relate this festival to *Punaladal* or confronting the freshes, mentioned in Sangam literature. A poem in *Paripadal* describes this festival: men are proceeding to the river on horseback and women are getting ready with sandal and turmeric for ceremonial bathing in preparation for the water festival.

In South India, it coincides with the Southwest monsoon that sets in July over the catchment areas in the Western Ghats, the fountainhead of all the Southern rivers. By mid-July, all the rivers swell up and are in spate.

The river at this stage is looked upon as a metaphor for a pregnant woman. And just as an expectant mother is entitled for all her favourite food, the devotees drop one handful of each type of rice into the river and only then sit down for their meal. Newly married couples – the wedding would have taken place in the month of *Aani* or *Vaikasi* – go together to the riverside. On this day, women replace the cotton *thali* (the sacred thread) with a golden chain or at least some gold is added to the new thread and the old one thrown into the river. Special prayers are made for the gift of a child.

Another feature of the festival is water-related games. Water-throwing, ranging from a courteous sprinkle or a polite splash to complete drenching, is done in a festive spirit. Spray guns made of freshly cut bamboo are on sale by the roadside a few days before the festival. For two or three days, we would be soaked in water throughout the day.

Writer Krishangini, also raised in a village on the banks of Amaravathi, wrote a Tamil short story titled "Three Inches Flood". It revolves around an old woman who comes from a village to her son's home in Chennai and spends the eighteenth of *Aadi*, waiting for water supply. Meanwhile, she recalls her younger days and the festival. It is a poignant story about the drying of Tamil Nadu rivers and an indictment on the way we have squandered our natural heritage.

This water festival of *Aadi* that has been a feature in our life for millennia cannot be celebrated any more as there are no more water flowing in the rivers. We have cleared our rain forests in the Western Ghats, created green deserts of tea and coffee plantations, wood-panelled our conference halls and built dams, drowning vast stretches of primeval forests and blocking the flow of rivers. All the springs have dried up there and the rivers in the plains are now mere scars on the face of Earth.

At the Citizens' meeting, we decided to buy a truckload of water and observe the festival near the dried up temple tank of Tiruvanmiyur.

–

The Hindu
(2001)

Language And Ecology: A Fading Heritage

"The two-way relation (of languages) to ecology needs to be developed. While discussing ecological issues, languages need to become part of the agenda."

David Crystal, in his book **Language Death**

We came out of the Rest house in Thekkady and saw our guide for the forest walk, Vediyappan, waiting for us. In olive greens, a pair of binoculars around his neck, he looked professional. A poacher-turned forest-guide, he had been assigned to us because he could speak Tamil. His knowledge of birds and plants was astounding. He pointed to a crimson-throated barbet and said it was called *kazhutharuthaan*, meaning one who had slit his throat, a name that describes a distinct feature of the bird. During the seven kilometres walk through the forest that January morning, we learnt the local names of many birds.

In any old civilization, the name of a bird or a mammal is not a mere word; it is a package of natural history information. It tells us something about that creature, either its appearance, its call or the habitat. The Tamil name for Fox is *Kuzhi nari* because it lives in a warren, while the jackal (*nari*) lives over ground. Some names describe the behaviour of the creature. The Marathi word for bat is *Vattavagul* meaning the one that roosts in the banyan. In Malayalam, the Great pied hornbill is *Malamuzhakki* (one who shakes the mountain). Anyone who has heard the noise of this massive bird taking off from a tree in the stillness of the forest will agree how apt the name is. When people live close to nature, they build up a specialized knowledge of aspects of the external world that surrounds them – animals, birds and plants – and this knowledge gets distilled and expresses itself in their language.

But we are losing these traditional nomenclatures fast. Not just the names, but proverbs and similes connected with these life forms, with nature, all are being lost as the conservation discourse is carried on in English. The legends and fables featuring these creatures are fading away. Indian languages are rich in metaphors relating to different life forms. "When metaphors die, ideas pass away and a way of thinking is buried," says a linguist.

The British have done immense work during the colonial days in the field of Natural History in India. But when it came to names of birds and mammals, they coined them from their point of view, like "Indian Robin", completely ignoring local names. They called a bird which has nothing to do with pheasant family as "Crow pheasant". M. Krishnan, writing in 1958, asked, "Who was responsible for calling our Gaur, wholly unrelated to the Bison family, the Bison? Who named the Tahr of the South, the Nilgiri Ibex? Who coined the utterly misleading name, Lion-tailed monkey, for one of our most distinctive macaques? The British 'gentleman sportsman' was responsible for all these misnomers, and besides some quite wretched natural history." A Kaani tribal in Kalakad-Mundandhurai sanctuary tells us that the Tamil name of Lion-tailed monkey is *Solaimandhi* – the monkey of the rainforest – as different from *Karumandhi* (the Black monkey, Nilgiri Langur).

So we inherited these names as a legacy of the British Raj. When they do not know the local name of an animal or a bird, our friends in the media and in Government departments take the shortcut of providing a literal translation of the English name instead of some effort to learn the original name. For example, King Cobra is literally translated as *Raja Naagam*, while its Tamil name is *Karunaagam* (black cobra). Ant-eater is another example. Its Tamil name is *Alangu*. The use of English words or their translation, in the place of local language, not only fails to communicate with the people, it also impoverishes the language. A heritage is being lost. Names that have been in use for millennia are thus getting forgotten. A whole new generation is growing up disconnected with nature. The umbilical cord with its heritage and culture has been cut. This of course is related to English being the medium of instruction. But that is another story.

This is one of the many reasons why the conservation movement has not become a people's movement and bird watching as a hobby is restricted largely to the English knowing group. The ideas and concepts of conservation have not been taken to the people in a language they understand. In all my birding years, I have observed that only in Gujarat do birders use local names. One of the earliest translations of Salim Ali's *Book of Indian Birds* was in Guajarati.

Traditional nomenclature, in each local language, should be redeemed and brought into parlance. This has become even more important because we have introduced environmental science in our schools. These names and metaphors will be very handy in the teaching of ecological concepts.

Not just names of birds, but of mammals, reptiles, trees, seasons and the terms connected with the external world that surrounds us, need to be redeemed. When I say "redeemed" I am not talking about dipping into ancient literature. I am talking about what is in vogue today in the villages. My observation is that many of these traditional names are still in use in rural areas. It is in urban areas that they have gone out of parlance. Many Tamil names of creatures have been forgotten by sheer neglect and apathy.

Take for example the term dolphin. These mammals have been close to humans for thousands of years, long before the English-speaking seafarers landed in our coast. Surely, we have a name for it? If you go and ask the fisherfolk in Santhome, Chennai they will tell you. But in the media, it is always dolphin. Many years ago, while strolling in the Zoology gallery of the Madras museum, I saw a skeleton of a dolphin mounted on the wall with the legend in Tamil *Oongil.* That is the Tamil name for the creature.

The Tamil names of many birds that have gone out of use here survive in Sri Lanka. In fact, G. M. Henry, in his *Guide to the Birds of Ceylon* (1971), documents these names which are still in use there. It is good news that in recent years we have at least two books, field guides for birds, in Tamil. One is *Thamizhnaattu Paravaikal* by Ka. Rathnam (2002); the other is the Tamil version of the *Field Guide to Indian Birds* by Richard Grimmett (2009).

If Tamil nomenclature, both for birds and mammals, are brought into use, it will facilitate spreading ecological concepts and winning public support for conservation movement. Redeeming the traditional names has become even more important as environmental science has been introduced in our schools. So to teach children we need books in local languages. Most of the books we have on wildlife are in English. It is in the urban areas, where important decisions are made and where policies are framed, that they have gone out of parlance

If a researcher is familiar with the Tamil names, she can delve into ancient or medieval literature and arrive at the provenance of bird species. The poets of ancient Tamil Nadu documented their external world with great detail. In describing backdrops to their narration they wrote about birds, mammals and plants. Here is an example, a poem written in Circa 3-4 AD, and attributed to the poet of Sathimutham village.

O stork, O stork, O red-legged stork
With coral-red beak, sharp tapered

Like the split tuber of the sprouting palmyra,
Should you and your spouse turn northward
From sojourning at the southern
Waters of Kanyakumari,
Halt at the tank of my village Sathimutham
And there seek out my wife,
In our wet-walled drip-thatched abode,
Listening to the gecko's whinnying voice
For augury of my return
and tell her that you saw this wretch
in Madurai, city of our Pandya king,
Grown thin with no clothes against the North-wind's bite
Hugging his torso with his arms,
Clasping his body with his upraised legs,
Barely existing, like the snake within its basket.

(Translated by M. Krishnan)

This poem gives a detailed description of the White stork, a winter migrant, and the name by which it is referred to in the poem – *Sengal narai* (Red-legged Stork) – is still in use. The poem also talks about the lizard, whose calls are still attributed with prophetic qualities and the captive snake. Krishnan cites another example, this time from *Kurinji – p-pattu,* line 219, which refers to the bird *anril,* known as Black Ibis in English. The poet records that in the evening "curve-beaked anril arrive at the broad-leaved tops of tall palmyrahs and make their calling sounds." Krishnan continues that while driving in Ramanathapuram area, he saw some Black ibises. He asked the name of the bird from some villagers by the roadside and they responded "anril". The old name is still in parlance. This could be true of the names of many other birds and animals.

In some Tamil novels of recent times, many natural history terms have been documented. Perumal Murugan's *Seasons of the Palm/ Koolamadhaari* springs to mind. Cho. Dharman, in his novel *The Owl/ Koogai* mentions the Tamil names of many birds. This is a heritage that needs to be conserved, not just the creatures but also their names.

–

(Michael Lockwood Endowment Lecture delivered on August 2005 at Madras Christian College, Tambaram)

Me, My Dog And The World Around

One of the problems with people today is that most of them deal only with lifeless, artificial objects in their daily work, with objects that are not particularly beautiful and that are by no means appropriate to inspire awe and respect. That's why most people have forgotten how to live with living creatures, with living systems.

-Konrad Lorenz in *On Life and Living*.

Recently, a friend sought my help in getting a license from wildlife authorities to keep a pet Bonnet macaque. She was working in a hospice, interacting with terminally ill people. She told me how, whenever she visited the hospice with her pet, the mere sight of that monkey brought cheer to the twenty odd inmates of the place. Such is the moment when a human re-establishes her/his relationship with another life form. Such a relationship with the other creatures that share with us this earth as home can be therapeutic. This – what is often referred to as 'pet therapy' – is now a recognized method of treatment among therapists.

This affinity with Nature and fellow creatures is part of our genetic makeup. When we start living in cities and lose ourselves in the time structure of our busy lives, this connection is destroyed. We stand alienated from Nature, so most of us pass through life as if the external world and other life forms do not exist at all. Trees, birds, butterflies, the sky, stars and clouds: all go unnoticed as we scurry through life in search of wealth and status. Psychotherapists opine that one of the characteristics of emotionally healthy human beings is that they love the natural world. They respond to sunsets, mountains, rivers and lakes. Aware of the external world that surrounds them, they realize that many creatures share this world. To put it briefly, they have a relationship with Nature. When this tie snaps, problems arise.

Nobel-prize winning ethologist Konrad Lorenz says that one can demonstrate easily that anyone who is bereft of genuine values spent his/ her childhood far removed from Nature. He goes on to add that anyone who has spent time in the countryside, snorkeled in a coral reef or wandered in a forest is very unlikely to be a slave to money and social positions. He advocates a process of deurbanization to counter this effect and regain emotional wellbeing.

Even while being a city dweller, we could redeem and retain our relationship with Nature by just being conscious of the many dimensions of nature in the urbanscape. You could have an aquarium at home with pet fish as part of your daily life. If you have space, maintain a garden, and if you do not have open space, potted plants can bring you closer to Nature. In most cities there are groups interested in Nature and conservation and one could join them. Even individually, one could develop sensitivity to Nature by learning to identify trees, birds and butterflies.

Birdwatching as a hobby is an interesting way of recreating this lost link with Nature. It is just an extension of the simple pleasure of looking at a bird. An interest in birds leads on to other areas such as conservation and environment and you soon realize that your concerns relating to Nature are widening into areas such as environmental issues and conservation. You begin to recognize the co-tenants in your home, such as the gecko on the wall or the Jumping spider you spot in your study. Pets can redeem the connection we lost with Nature.

One simple way to keep in touch with animals is to keep pets. It could be a parrot, cat or even a goat. I see the dog as a bridge between the world of humans and the world of other creatures, including animals. Ethologists point out that it is dog that was domesticated first. They say that being so clever, dog has figured out that it is man who has dominion over the resources of Earth and if only it could attach itself to humans, it will be taken care of. I am not sure how sound this theory is. But dogs connect their masters with the world of other creatures and also develop a sensibility to other creatures in their owners.

The best time to forge a relationship with nature is during childhood. One of my most pleasant memories of parenting is taking our two children on nature walks in the wilderness. Often their friends would join us in the trips. That is when I learnt that it is easy to teach children about ecological systems and create in them a respect for Nature. Once the spark is ignited, it glows throughout one's life. We were fortunate to live in places where forests were close by: Shillong, Coimbatore and Bengaluru. The children soon formed a club, which they called Walden Nature Club, and organized one-day treks and weekend camps. Many of this club's members have made careers in environment related fields. The others continue to nurture their relationship with Nature, in whichever part of the world they are.

I was fortunate to spend my childhood, shared with two sisters and two brothers, in a village by a perennial river. When we were not in school, we spent much of our waking hours out in the open, either on trees or in the river. There were days when we joined the man who went about poking the soil at the water's edge with a long pole to locate mud turtles.

On one side of the village was a scrubland, which we roamed for hours on end. In addition to the different varieties of snakes, we would come across jackals and hares. The night sky was full of stars and the Milky Way could clearly be seen. The tie we forged with Nature continued to provide zest to my life. My own relationship with Nature and wildlife is intuitive. For me the sight of a bull gaur emerging from forest cover – like an ebony carving on the move – into the grassland lit by a golden sun is a transcendental experience. To me, wild creatures symbolize the external world and my link with it. I delight in observing a bird through my binoculars and I feel part of the vast network of life forms.

–

The Hindu

(2004)

SAVING INDIA'S WILDLIFE: TWO PERSPECTIVES

These are good times for readers of books on Natural History; the two new books being reviewed here are the latest in the list of impressive works by experts in the field. The days when nature lovers had to rely on yarns spun by hunters have gone. Now we have authentic, scientific and reliable writing. These books exemplify wildlife biologists' contribution to our understanding of the dynamics of conservation.

We could identify broadly two types of wildlifers in our country: those for whom wildlife is a grist to the academic mill and career and who will not care if the last Hangul [Kashmir stag (*Cervus canadensis hanglu*)] is shot out of existence. Wildlife studies has emerged as an attractive field and there is a rush to get into this now. For them, conservation may, as Karanth writes, "be another nine-to-five job." The other, on the basis of the insights gained as wildlifers, stick their necks out, take on the establishment and often pay a price for it. Karanth clearly belongs to the second category. Whether it is questioning the method used in tiger census or the debate on people versus sanctuaries, he has been clear in his position. The stand he has taken on such issues has gotten him involved protracted legal battles.

An autobiographical structure binds together *A View from the Machan*, in which Karanth explains his philosophy of conservation. It is a biocentric one. "I am deeply concerned that wildlife and wild lands, which have evolved over millions of years must survive on this planet at least in their present remnant form; I believe that the present generation of humans has no moral right to extirpate wild nature and that we hold nature in trust for future generations." Right from the beginning, as he details in the first chapter, his interest lies in protecting the tiger and devising methods of conservation suitable to Indian conditions. This seems to have been the motivational force behind all his works.

Starting from his childhood in South Karnataka, Karanth traces the early influences of books and ideas and provides us with word portraits of individuals who influenced him. His father, Gnanapeeth award winner, Shivaram Karanth and Kenneth Anderson are described in detail. He then moves on to his work, his concerns and his ideology; though the focus is on tiger, he talks about other predators and the problems of conservation in India.

Later, he mentions forest official Chinnappa who introduced Karanth into the mysteries and thrills of bush craft. He writes in detail about Chinnappa's tenure in Nagerahole, which has come to be recognized as a singular success story.

In the Nagerahole initiative, Chinnappa and others persuaded the locals to take up responsibility for the wildlife in their area. This turned out to be the key to the success in preservation of wildlife in that sanctuary. In this effort, Chinnappa had to face powerful opponents and harassment which at least once found him behind bars for a trumped-up murder charge. But in the end, he was able to win the trust and goodwill of people around the sanctuary.

Karanth writes about coming into contact with wildlife biologists like Mel Sunquist and John Seidensticker and how it changed his life. What strikes the reader is his single- minded pursuit.

After learning radio-tracking method, he radio-collared a few tigers in Nagerahole. This was the first time in India that this method was employed, and it extended the frontiers of wildlife research. His detractors started an unseemly controversy in the press about this technique and many wildlifers exposed their abysmal ignorance by participating in this debate. However, the method of radio-tracking proved its worth and soon it was in use to study the lions of Gir and the elephants in Mudumalai also. Now a young primatologist is planning to radio-track Slender lorises.

In this work, Karanth once again demonstrates his remarkable powers of description. In the world he creates for readers, not just big cats, but jungle fowl, giant squirrels and langurs come alive. He sketches in charming details like the atmosphere around a waterhole as he waits for the animals to appear. Karanth's strong emotional tie to wildlife comes through in his writings. His main focus has been Nagerahole, located in one of the world's richest regions in biodiversity.

As a wildlife biologist, Karanth interprets the happenings in the jungle in the larger backdrop of survival of species. While he has his distinct style, this aspect of his writing reminds me of Schaller and endows his writing with an extra dimension. When a leopard comes across three dholes, it flees at first sight, without even seeing if it was a large pack; Karanth observes that, in evolutionary terms, this action of the cat had greater survival value. He adds that this capability to survive is the reason behind its wide provenance, from Africa to the Far East.

Karanth strongly believes that the tools provided by modern technology, such as radio-tracking through satellites, are a boon to conservation and wildlife research. He argues for a closer coordination between wildlife research and management of sanctuaries.

The heart of this book is on tiger conservation, which is tied up with the well-being of other creatures of the jungle. Writing about one of the animals radio-collared by Karanth – tigress Sundari of

Nagerhole – George Schaller writes in his Foreword, "Here is one of the most wonderful expressions of life on earth and it lifts our spirits. In an age when Nature is being viewed mainly in terms of natural resources, in dollar values, my heart speaks to Sundari. She is a strong reminder that conservation is also a moral issue of assuring other beings on this planet their right to exist."

It is appropriate that A. J. T. Johnsingh has titled his book *Field days*. He has made his mark as a wildlife biologist in field work and his students, in different parts of the world, excel in field work and adore him as a teacher. The book is a collection of his thirty-seven articles, published in newspapers and scientific journals, the oldest going back to 1972. The reader can discern the growth of the author as a writer and as a wildlife biologist. In this book, he shares his experience and insights. The articles on the wildlife of North Eastern India, in Mizoram, Meghalaya and Arunachal Pradesh, are particularly valuable and provide the reader with fascinating details not usually available.

In the rest of India, almost all the major sanctuaries have been covered, including Moondradaipu, the little known heronry near Tirunelveli. We read an insider's account of the search for a second home for the Asiatic lion and how the Kuno sanctuary was chosen. His coverage of the sanctuaries in the other Eastern countries throw open a new area to readers. Readers get fascinating accounts of little-known habitats like the Arakan mountain ranges of Myanmar, home to the second largest wild population of the Asiatic elephant. The piece on the Gibbon sanctuary in Thailand is a rare account of the evergreen forests in that part of the world. The problems of conservation in war-torn Vietnam reminds the reader of Kashmir.

One advantage an author gets in anthologizing articles is that he can expand the points he had touched upon in the article, because there is no constraint on the length in a book. But this advantage has not been utilized here. Johnsingh has merely added short postscripts to some pieces. Similarly, while putting the articles in book form, one needs to double check the facts. A book comes in for closer scrutiny than a newspaper article. For instance, Black buck were not introduced in the Guindy National Park, as the author says in his 1976 article; they are the original inhabitants of that stretch of coastal scrub jungle. During the tenure of the Raja of Bhavnagar as Governor, chital were introduced into this habitat from a small population that was in the Government Estate at Mount Road. Correctness and consistency in spelling of place names is another area that needs attention in a collection of articles written in different periods.

Book designing is a discipline which does not get adequate attention in India. The other day I was talking to a successful publisher about employing a book designer. He thought I was talking about cover designs. In *Field Days*, there is a small, dark square on top of each page, the purpose of which is not clear. Stamp size photographs serve no purpose. It is sad that we have passed the black & white phase of photography. Digital B&W pictures lack contrast and appear flat and devoid of sharpness. I wonder if we can ever redeem the tonal value of conventional B&W photos.

Aimed at non-specialists, these books are sure to win new converts to the gospel of conservation. Both books contain useful bibliographies, though an index is sorely missing. It would have increased the worth of these books even more. However, *Field Days* contains an exhaustive list of creatures mentioned in the book. Had the page numbers in which they appear been given, it would have served as a useful index.

One last point. Both the writers completed their schooling in regional language medium. Karanth, in fact, started writing in Kannada first. Yet their English writing is so readable and expressive, a good example to point out to those who cannot make a distinction between proficiency in one language and medium of instruction.

–

Frontline

(2003)

A View from the Machan: How Science Can Save the Fragile Predator,

By K. Ullas Karanth. Permanent Black, New Delhi. 2006. Hard cover. Pages 153.

Price Rs.350

Field days: A Naturalist's Journey through South and Southeast Asia by A. J. T. Johnsingh, Universities Press. Hyderabad, 2006. Pages 340 paperback. Price Rs. 350

A pregnant Tiger crossing the road

A jackal killed on the road

Tiger tourism

Sloth Bear with cubs

Nilgiri Langur

Leopard

White-Bellied Sea Eagle

Also by S. Theodore Baskaran

The Dance of the Sarus. Wanderings of a naturalist. Oxford University Press. 1997 Hard cover Price.

The Sprint of the Black Buck. Writings on Wildlife and Conservation in South India.(ED) Penguin Books. 2010 Rs. 299.

The Book of Indian Dogs. Aleph Book Company. 2017, Hard cover. Rs. 399

My Native Land Essays on Nature by M.Krishnan. (Ed with A.Rangarajan). Indus Source Books. 2019. Rs.499.

Photo credits

Bharathidasan

Ian Lockwood

Jayaraman, Tiruchi

John Isaac

Kalyan Varma

Lokanathan.L.

Nithila Baskaran

Peter Rae

Priya Davidar

Raveendran Natarajan

Saket Badola

Shiela Castelino

Sri kantha R G

Vjay cavale

Index

A

B

C

J

K

M

N

O

P

Q

R

S

T

V

W

Y

Z

www.ingramcontent.com/pod-product-compliance
Ingram Content Group UK Ltd.
Pitfield, Milton Keynes, MK11 3LW, UK
UKHW041630190726
13854UKWH00006B/2404